A Seemingly Unfillable Heart

AN ADOPTION JOURNEY

GINA CROTTS

This is a work of creative nonfiction. The events and conversations are portrayed to the best of Gina Crotts' memory. While all the stories in this book are true, all names and identifying details have been changed to protect the privacy of the people involved.

Copyright © 2019 by Gina Crotts

All rights reserved. No part of this book may be reproduced or used in any manner without the written permission of the copyright owner except for the use of quotations in a book review.

First paperback edition 2019

Book design by Gina Crotts
Edited by Sarah Winn

ISBN : 9781689197328

Published by 1901 Publishing
www.ginacrotts.com

ACKNOWLEDGEMENTS

To my parents, your guidance and support, during this time, gave me the confidence to move forward.

To my friends, your unconditional love was imperative.

To my husband, your shoulder has always been there for me to cry on, thank you for believing in me.

To my four children, you inspire me every day to become a better person. I love you!

CHAPTER ONE
Positive 8

CHAPTER TWO
Choosing Adoption   16

CHAPTER THREE
Face to Face   28

CHAPTER FOUR
My Little Butterfly   35

CHAPTER FIVE
The Handoff   46

CHAPTER SIX
Birth Mother Baskets   63

CHAPTER SEVEN
Dear, Grief   79

CHAPTER EIGHT
Post Placement   89

CHAPTER NINE
Happy Birthday   106

CHAPTER TEN
The End of a Fairytale   120

CHAPTER ELEVEN
The Square   124

CHAPTER TWELVE
A Full Heart   131

AUTHOR'S NOTE

When you feel called to do something and that something feels bigger than anything you could imagine, it takes what I call "Lion Courage" to fulfill the task. For me, writing this book was very much this way. After suffering a severe concussion, I found peace in meditation. After each meditation, I would journal, and often wrote: "I am a writer." I have always wanted to share my adoption story in book form but lacked the courage to do so.

Finding my Lion Courage meant silencing the lies that had evolved into personal beliefs about myself and my-so-called limitations. It also required some in-depth soul searching that I wondered whether I could even survive emotionally. Certain fears never left me, even to this day, but how I reacted to the fear changed everything!

A Seemingly Unfillable Heart does not differ from many birth mother's stories—it is a story about courage, grief, love, and growth. My wish is that you find your Lion Courage to become what you are called to be.

I believe the events that took place in this book were pre-designed for me to make such a decision. I am not here to make a judgment on others' choices, and I believe everyone should have the right to choose their path.

The most courageous act is to become what is whispered to you when you are still.

ONE

Positive

Broken girls blossom into warriors.

I laid back and let my entire body sink into the bubbles. I have always said that I do my best thinking while soaking in a hot bath, but tonight I wasn't thinking. I was praying. The double red lines on my pregnancy test kept appearing in my mind, like flashing neon lights. Positive. Positive. Positive.

That $6.99 plastic stick revealed everything about me: my past, my future, and the label I would carry for the rest of my life. I didn't need a mirror. That stick showed my reflection perfectly, a teenage pregnancy, a statistic.

I dunked my head completely under the water. *I'm fine. I can do this. It's okay. I'll be okay.* By the time my head resurfaced, I was sobbing again. I'd try and stop myself, sliding my body deep into the water and again telling myself, *I can do this. I'm okay. I'll be okay.* But every time I resurfaced, my emotions would break through.

I stepped out of the tub and grabbed a damp towel without bothering to dry off. I wrapped every inch of my body inside the towel and curled up in my twin bed that was resting on cinder blocks. I lay there overcome by the battle in my mind between positive, encouraging thoughts and the depths of fear. These emotions bounced back and forth like a Ping-Pong ball on a tennis table. Never before had I found myself with such contrasting feelings of courage and angst.

My college life was not filled with goals of who and what I wanted to become. It was how fast and whom I would marry. This was the culture in which I was raised. Growing up, I knew few women who had careers and worked outside of the home, and it was unusual to see women who had aspirations other than raising a family.

This is the same community that I believed would shun me for having premarital sex. I stayed in an unhealthy relationship for over two years, because of that fear. I rationalized my actions by telling myself that since we were getting married, somehow what we were doing was less "sinful." If the end result were marriage, maybe I would still be accepted as a faithful member of my community and religion.

The next few weeks, as the truth unfolded, thoughts and emotions began to unravel for everyone involved. My friends and family were both supportive and devastated. It wasn't but a few weeks into my pregnancy that I realized they would be the only ones by my side during this trying time. But even with their support, the biggest decision of my life was entirely up to me.

GROWING UP AS A Latter-day Saint (LDS), more commonly known as "Mormon", we attended church every Sunday as a family. More often than not, I attended alone without my siblings. My sister closest in age to me, but still five years older, discounted the church at the age of thirteen. That same year, at eight years old, I officially became a member of the LDS church. My older two siblings were already married and attending their own congregations, referred to in the church as "wards." The church created geographical boundaries around neighborhoods. If you lived within certain boundaries, you were required to attend church at a set time and building, as a member of a specified ward.

In my teen years, I was also required to go to Young Women's activities once a week. I was taught that my body is a temple, and I should not allow any unclean thing inside its pure, white temple walls. This included drugs, alcohol, coffee, tea, and the greatest sin, premarital sex. I was taught that I would be considered impure or "chewed up goods" for my future husband if I lost my virginity to another, before marriage. I was taught to follow the commandments and my life would be blessed for doing so. If I didn't follow them, my life would be full of trials, difficulties, and unhappiness.

I was also taught about modesty in dress. My artistic nature never seemed to fit into what the church considered a modest way of dressing and presenting yourself. I continuously felt like a square peg forcing myself into a round hole. I noticed my parent's enthusiasm and sense of pride in me when I accomplished anything that was tied to our church. I was thirsty for their approval and acceptance, even more so because I felt a lack of acceptance coming from my religious community. I was different enough to notice I wasn't a part of the whole, but common enough to be engaged with my fellow church members.

The church taught me that a life of sin would be followed with a life of punishment. Those who did not believe as we did never found true happiness. Follow the straight and narrow, and you will be eternally blessed; don't, and you will be punished. I was fully aware of the ramifications in our community if you openly strayed from the church's standards. If the shame of your own sins wasn't enough to scare you into a sin-free life, the judgment from your ward members would force you to obey.

The horrifying thought of telling my parents I was pregnant was paralyzing. I knew I would be crushing their idealistic view of what my future looked like. I was certain a teenage pregnancy was not on their top ten list of things I would accomplish. Nor was it on mine. I had dramatically changed the course of my life. The tracks only ran in one direction and there was no room for me to jump on a fresh trail, though every bone in my body ached to board a different train. I was pregnant, and the only delivery I could think about was that of delivering the dreadful news to my parents.

MY MOTHER AND I have one thing in common: We love to shop. What we were shopping for that night is far from my memory, but the drive home was unforgettable.

"Mom, I'm pregnant," I blurted out as we drove around the Point of the Mountain.

She was neither shocked nor dramatic in her reply. She simply kept driving as if I had made a statement about the weather. I gazed out the passenger door window, watching the cars pass by, awaiting her response. I yearned to be in any passenger seat but this one, to be anyone other than who I was in that moment. I wanted to slurp the words back into my mouth, swallow them until they were digested so far down in my gut that they were no longer my reality.

Say something! I silently screamed.

When I felt like my declaration had gone unheard, I adjusted my seat back and leaned into the awkward, unknown silence. I didn't have the grit to repeat those words.

As we exited the freeway, she finally spoke. "What are you going to do?"

A confident response here felt not only vital but also extremely important considering my mom's view of my maturity. After all, if I was mature enough to be having sex, I should be mature enough to know what to do with the consequences. I fished for the right words to ease the blow, for both of us, but nothing was biting. The road leading home was also the path to the Point of the Mountain; it was lined with open fields and rolling hills. The stretch felt like an hour instead of the usual fifteen minutes. I found myself eagerly helping my mom look for deer, fearing that I had shocked her enough that she may hit one on the ride home.

"I'm not sure what I'm going to do," I managed to say.

"Well, where is Justin? What does he have to say about all of this?" her question trailing off into a pool of sarcasm. Justin was my boyfriend—the boyfriend my parents disapproved of—and the birth father.

She knew Justin didn't care about me, which I was also quickly learning. I didn't bother to answer a question we both knew the answer to.

"Will you tell dad?" I begged.

"Absolutely not. You will," she said firmly.

My mother was wise in choosing her words, waiting for my father's response. Most of their marriage ran this way, especially when it came to weighty decisions. Neither one was quick to reply without the other's opinion or judgment. They often discussed things together and then showed a united front.

We traveled the deer infested road back to my parent's house where my father awaited our arrival, and I prepared to light the fuse on the massive war bomb I was about to drop in the middle of his lap.

A two-toned wood kitchen table set adjacent to

two windows that faced the side of our neighbor's home. There was no view there, but I found myself charmed by those windows. I gazed in their direction as I sat quietly in a chair next to my father. He was sitting at the head of the table, and I was sitting to his left. His arms were relaxed and crossed on the tabletop, his toes touching the floor but his heels off of the ground. He didn't look like he was expecting a bomb; in fact, he looked the complete opposite, eager to listen.

"Your mom said you want to talk to me about something?" he asked in his monotone way.

I shuffled my feet below me, creating vacuum like marks up and down the carpet. I wanted to skirt around the question. I held the lighter in my hand with the bomb fuse waving back and forth in my face. It was taunting me to light it up, but I refused, wanting instead to drop it and run out the door. I looked at my father, his sincere demeanor, and his baby like face staring back at me. I ached to turn back time. I would give anything to be his baby girl again, the one who spent hours playing basketball with him out on the driveway. I wanted to watch him move the cars out of the way and park them along the road, so we'd have enough space for a game of H.O.R.S.E. I wanted to plunge myself back to playing Barbie's in my room and listening to Casey Kasem's Top 40 on the radio. The innocent way that he looked at me, as if I could conquer the world, was about to blow up in our faces.

"I'm pregnant, dad," I finally blurted out. And just like that, I lit that damn taunting fuse, leaned back, squinted my eyes shut and cringed as I waited for the boom of the explosion, but there was nothing. Not even a small backfire. His tone neither changed nor his demeanor. I opened my eyes slowly to see him simply nod.

I pulled my arms far enough into my oversized flannel shirt to wrap them around my mid-section. I sulked as I headed to my car and drove back to my apartment. I passed my roommates without saying a word, shut my bedroom door, smothered my face into my down pillow, and sobbed. I cried in shame. I cried for my sins, and I cried about the way God was clearly punishing me. I cried for the innocent way in which my father always doted on me, and I cried about how I would miss his endearing expression. He didn't need to say anything. His troublesome nod and the expression on his face confirmed my every fear. From this point forward, I believed I would no longer be clean, not only for my future husband, but in the eyes of my entire community. I was a disgrace.

TWO

Choosing Adoption

"I'm going to make everything around me beautiful-that will be my life." –Elsie De Wolfe

"*This* plastic tube is inserted, and the vacuum begins," she instructed as she held up a 1" diameter tube. "The pregnancy tissue will flow through the tube and out of your body."

It was another ordinary day in high school, or so I thought. I had no idea this presentation would be something I'd look back on as one of the most pivotal moments in my life. I found myself drifting off into my thoughts for the first half hour until the presenter lifted up that tube and described the vacuum-like effect. It felt gruesome to me. My seventeen-year-old ears heard the presentation like this: You insert this large plastic tube into your vagina (ouch) and you suck out the baby parts using this vacuum (gross).

"Your other option is adoption," the lady announced. She was five minutes into completing her hour-long presentation. It was the first time I thought about the word adoption and the first time she had said it that day. It was exceptionally quiet for a room full of high school juniors. Also unusual was that I sensed no bias in the room. No one was arguing that abortion is right or wrong, which was especially weird considering the religious majority in the room staunchly opposed abortion.

I rested my arms across the wood desktop as I watched the presenter pack up her supplies. The impatience of the students grew around me as they awaited the school bell. But I felt no urgency. Somewhere, I was contemplating my options. There was no religious pressure. Although I knew where the majority stood, I felt free to consider what I believed. The bell alerted the mass of students to exit their classrooms. I grabbed my backpack, threw it on my back and said to myself, *I would choose adoption.*

"You have to get up." My sister nudged me. "You can't lay in this bed any longer. Get up and get going. Your wallowing isn't helping." Her words were stern.

I had been lying in my bed for weeks, feeling sorry for myself, for this new person I had become. I didn't want to go out. I was chewed up, used goods.

A SEEMINGLY UNFILLABLE HEART

The fear that I had fallen away from the path of true happiness imprisoned me.

My stomach had begun to take shape. There was no hiding the scarlet letter that had sewn itself to my chest. I was a disgrace to my community, to myself, to my religion, and to my family. I had failed to keep myself clean, to save myself for my prince charming who was going to race in on his galloping horse. I had failed as a member of my church, as a daughter, as a daughter of God, and as a future wife. *"Who would want me now?"* I thought.

After the rest of my family found out about my mother-to-be status, I moved back to my parents' house. I hauled my belongings out of my college dorm, to the parking lot and into Red, my cherry red Ford truck, like a six-year-old who got caught stealing gum at the convenience store. I was ashamed and embarrassed to have failed at my first attempt at being on my own. I was now moving back in with my parents, like a child, to the exact place I was so eager to leave.

"You got caught. So what?" my sister asked. I looked at her confused. "How many girls your age are having sex? How many Mormon girls are sinning?" she asked. "You're just the one who got caught, so face it and figure it out," she demanded.

The quaint bedroom in my parents' home had become my sanctuary. If I stayed there long enough, maybe this belly of mine would dissipate. If I prayed harder, if I promised never to sin again, maybe God would take it all away. I could go back to being a regular teenager again and could ignore the consequences of my reckless actions. I spent hours listening to soft tunes of the heartbroken and crying until nothing would release anymore. The world I created in that bedroom was the only place where I was safe, where I felt any amount of control over my life. I wasn't ready to face the world outside, where everyone would not only have an opinion of what I should do next but would see my uncleanliness.

My father kept his distance, hardly speaking to me since I had moved back home. I translated his silence as anger and hatred. Saying nothing at all meant, at least in my mind, that he had nothing good to say. I wasn't sure if I wanted him to spit in my face and scream at me about what a disgrace I was, or if the silent treatment was better. I would never know, and it didn't matter, since words were not exchanged. My internal self-loathing was punishment enough without the echoes of his silence.

My sister was determined to convince me to leave my haven. When I looked into her eyes, I didn't see shameful sympathy. I saw strength. I didn't see pity as I had received from others. I saw encouragement. I saw her confidence in me. And for the first time since I had seen those double red lines on that pregnancy test, I felt hopeful. She was right. I wasn't the only Mormon teenager who was sexually active or sinning. I was, however, the one who got caught, and I had to face that fact.

Her encouraging me to stand up and face the consequences and decisions that lay ahead was a turning point in my pregnancy. From that day forward, I no longer hid my sin. I would no longer be shameful but hopeful. I would not allow my religious preconceptions to make me feel like an outcast. I would stand up for the decisions I had made, as well as the decisions I was about to make, and I would stop feeling sorry for myself. I would stop worrying about how I was an embarrassment to my family and faith. I would stop acting like I was the only one who had ever sinned. I chose to rise above the stereotypes. I wasn't proud of who I was, but I was determined to move forward from my mistakes and turn them into something beautiful. I declared myself worthy enough to hold my head high even with no religious community behind me. There was still light, love, and courage inside of me. It only took encouragement from a single person to remind me: I can do this.

I HEARD MY DAD pull into the driveway. Red was now ready for departure. My heart both sank and leapt at the thought of starting my life somewhere new. My dad was returning from having a metal toolbox installed in the bed of my truck, so I could keep my belongings safe as my mother and I traveled the 550 miles to Arizona. I stuffed the toolbox with clothes, shoes, books, and journals, a real woman's' truckload. My mother packed a small bag and threw it in the back. She would help me get settled and then fly home alone.

I stood back astonished that everything that mattered to me now could fit into such a small space. Every article I left behind was of great importance at one time, but now my days of being a teenager were over. My tomorrow was a new life in Arizona, with decisions to be made by an expectant mother.

A mother.

I had never yearned to be a mother. The daunting task frightened me. Regardless of my fear, or my age, regardless of whether I was equipped for this or not, it was going to happen. It didn't matter what I packed in my truck. I was headed on a road trip, and the final destination was not only the desert hills where I would be living, it was motherhood.

My choice to move to Arizona, to live with my brother, was just that, *my* choice. After spending weeks in the tiny room in my parent's house, and thanks to my sister's encouragement, I was ready for a change. Subconsciously, I was escaping the judgment of my community — I didn't want to face my peers — but at the forefront of my mind, I wanted to be on my own. I needed solitude to collect my thoughts and make decisions that would not be tainted by my surroundings or those closest to me.

My brother is eleven years older than me. He got married in 1990, when I was only ten-years-old. He moved to Arizona, and I didn't have much connection with him from then on. And yet, his decision to allow me to move in with him and his four children appeared to be an easy one. Looking back, I didn't think about how he might be judged by my moving in. After all, he was exposing his ward to his unfaithful sister who was now living in his home. I didn't think about how he might explain my situation to his young children, answering questions about why I was pregnant and not married. Ironically, I was not concerned about the pointing fingers of the new community of Mormons. I felt prepared and armed for my next step.

A SEEMINGLY UNFILLABLE HEART

Everything inside me knew this is where I should be. I knew I would find clarity in changing my environment, and my growing confidence made it easier to ignore the naysayers.

THE ARIZONA NIGHT SKY was clear as ice. Each star rang out its brilliance as I drove around in circles. This place had been home for two weeks now. I passed neighborhood after neighborhood, all with tile roofs and dry rock landscape. I had a decision to make, and I wasn't going to stop driving Red until I made it.

The heat rose off the black pavement, even with the sun resting below my view. I rolled down the driver's side window and let the heat blow through my hair. It helped clear my mind to feel the extreme opposites of the night sky and the 90-degree weather. I mentally started a list of pros and cons of parenting my baby and placing my baby for adoption.

PARENTING PROS

- I get to dress you in cute clothes and show you off to my friends.
- I won't have the pressure of picking the perfect family for you.
- I won't have to worry about you, where you are, or if you're being taken care of.
- I won't have to live my whole life without you.

- I will never have to say goodbye. I will never have to let you go, and you will always remember me.

PLACING PROS

- You will have a mom and a dad.
- You will have opportunities that I can't provide for you.
- You won't have to bounce back and forth from house to house, if Justin were to ever come back into the picture.
- You will be a beautiful gift for a couple who has waited so long to have a baby.

I pulled Red to the side of the road, sat back and contemplated my list of Parenting and Placing Pros. I noticed everything I listed for parenting my baby started with an "I," stating what I wanted or didn't want. The pros for placing my child for adoption all started with a "you." As the list grew, in my mind, I saw a stark difference between one that was solely benefiting me and one that was all for the benefit of my baby.

I closed my eyes and listened to the cars around me. They passed by with such speed. Each person was hustling to his or her next destination, each one passing me with no concept of me even being there, and there I was frozen in time. After months of deliberating, I knew what I had to do, and all I could do was grasp the seat belt across my chest and cry.

THREE

Face To Face

I met Ray on a Wednesday evening at a dance club called, The Omni. Every Wednesday evening was country night at The Omni. My roommates and I enjoyed the more relaxed feel there, instead of the weekend nights of clubbing. This particular Wednesday evening was no different than any other, except that my then boyfriend of two years, Justin, had broken up with me the night before. My roommates dragged me out in an attempt to lift my spirits. None of my roommates liked Justin. Our emotionally charged relationship of breaking up, getting back together, and breaking up again seemed to exhaust even my closest friends. By now, there was no sympathy from them when I would announce another break up. They were, however, eager for me to meet someone who would break the emotionally draining cycle.

My girlfriends and I often stood in a wolf pack on the dance floor, unaware of how difficult this made it for anyone to ask us to dance. We were engrossed in our little pack, the laughter and fun we always had together, when Ray approached the tribe. I was standing the furthest away from the dance floor and from him. He had to push through all of the femininity to get close enough for me to hear him. When he first parted the pack, I smiled, thinking about who he might ask to dance. It never crossed my mind that it would be me until he stretched his hand out towards me and asked, "Would you like to dance?"

We spent the remainder of the night dancing with each other as if no one else were at the club. Ray had this uncanny way of making me feel beautiful, not by the words he wooed me with, but the mere look on his face. I felt his delight in my presence. In his mind, he was dancing with the best girl in the room, and his assurance had me believing the same. After several dances, we exchanged numbers and discussed going out on a date soon.

Ray lived in the town adjacent to my hometown, though I did not know him growing up. He was eight years older than me. Ray, the oldest of four children, grew up riding horses down Main Street in the small farm town nearby. I had heard his name through mutual friends, but we had never officially met until the night at The Omni. Ray spent most of his youth playing baseball. His parents had a large batting cage on the left side of their house, taking up a majority of their backyard. He played a year of college ball and then had returned to his hometown to work with his father when we met.

Ray was considerably older than other boys I had dated. In the Mormon religion, young men leave for a church mission at the age of eighteen, returning two years later with the hope of marrying their eternal companion. If you were past the age of twenty-one and not engaged or married, you were in the minority. Ray was twenty-six when we met. He didn't serve a Mormon mission or feel moved by the pressure to marry young. My questioning instinct was intrigued by the fact that he didn't serve a mission. It felt almost courageous in a community full of blind followers.

The weekend after we met, I made the first bold move and called Ray. I was enthusiastic about getting to know him better. I dialed with no hesitation. I hoped he'd be happy to hear my voice, and I was eager to talk to him. I sat at the top of the stairs in my apartment, running my fingers through the plush, worn-down carpet on the top stair leading down into the basement where I slept. I sat on that step for four hours. Not one minute passed without an outburst of laughter at something hilarious that Ray said. He was funny, sincere, and we could talk for hours. Our quick friendship was effortless.

He seemed enamored with who I was. He admired my artistic ability and encouraged me to discover it in more depth. He wasn't egotistical like most of the boys I had dated previously. I found myself becoming more fully who I was instead of falling into the patterns and likes of whoever I was with. I could confidently be myself and felt no need to lean into who he was or what he liked for him to admire me.

Ray and I dated for four weeks when my exboyfriend, Justin, returned and pleaded for me to take him back. My relationship with Ray had barely begun, and the time we had spent together felt insignificant compared to the unintended bond I had already created with Justin. The pull of regretful sin has a way of altering what the heart truly wants and what the mind says you have to do. It was not a choice to return to Justin; it was more like an act of repentance, as if going back to that relationship was a way to earn God's forgiveness. It was my way of showing (and hoping) that my relationship with Justin wasn't actually sinful because I returned to him in hope of an acceptable marriage. I had done this over and over again. This was my fearful attempt to avoid a life of punishment, and though I felt more confidently myself as Ray's girlfriend, I saw no other way but to make amends with my past and break up with Ray. After Ray and I parted, I did not hear from him again.

I HEARD THE LANDLINE ring. I listened to my sister-in-law pick it up. I listened to her footsteps ascending the stairs and then entering my room. I had only been in Arizona for three short weeks before I received that phone call from Ray. I had decided to place my baby for adoption only a week prior.

A SEEMINGLY UNFILLABLE HEART

"Is this Gina?" the voice on the line asked.

"Yes, it is," I hesitantly replied.

"This is Ray. How are you?"

My heart sank. Was I happy to hear his voice? Did he call to rub my face in the choices I had made following our break up?

"I'm good. I'm surprised to hear from you. How did you get this number?"

"I ran into one of your friends. She told me you're pregnant," he blurted out.

The sentence made me cringe as it shot through the line. I was certain several people were running into each other and discussing my current state. The gossip and judgment that must be going on at home was something I had to push aside daily.

Here it comes, I thought. The pointing of fingers, the judgment of my sinful nature, the lecture I deserved.

"I haven't been able to stop thinking about you." We talked for three hours about where each of us had been in the time apart. As I went to hang up the phone I heard Ray say, "You know, you could keep the baby and I will help you. We could get married." He confidently stated.

I didn't hesitate in my response, "I'm placing her for adoption, Ray. I know it is what I am supposed to do."

His words lingered long after I hung up the phone with him. Every fiber of my being wanted to hear something similar from Justin, but I never did, and I never would. Every inch of my heart broke in half as I listened to my quick reply. I knew I had chosen the right path for her and for myself, but the longing to keep her didn't stop. It didn't stop Ray's tempting words from repeating themselves in my head throughout the rest of my pregnancy.

I HAD CHOSEN ADOPTION, and with that came choosing her parents. Before I picked Shawn and Alice as the couple to raise my child, I received a four-page document on their "stats" along with a handful of photos. I was presented with ten adoptive parent profiles, and Shawn and Alice were among the first ten I looked at. The process of picking a couple was overwhelming. It was the first time in the adoption process where I felt myself being defiant.

"Here are your couples," my social worker said as she slapped a stack of papers on the coffee table in front of me.

"Ok, thanks," I mumbled.

She stood there with her arms folded as I gazed up at her. *Was she going to stand there and wait for me to grab one out of the pile like I was picking a lottery ticket?* I thought. I took the stack and started reading what I call "stats," while she sat in the chair next to me. The "stats" looked like this:

Alice
  5'9"
  130 lbs
  DOB 1974
Shawn
  6'2"
  175 lbs
  DOB 1972

A SEEMINGLY UNFILLABLE HEART

"Stats" on every couple, times ten, and a few paragraphs about how they met, how long they had been waiting for a baby, and some family traditions. Each profile looked the same as the next; each couple walked the same, talked the same, and sounded the same. I recklessly grabbed four profiles, at random, and took them home with me. I couldn't do this with my social worker peering over me. Her curious eyes anticipating my choice made me feel like I was an animal at the zoo, like she was waiting for me to scratch my butt or make some silly face.

I envied every couple I looked at. They all portrayed a happy, healthy relationship. The only thing they were missing was a child. You know what I was missing? A partner who cared about the baby I was carrying, his baby, his flesh and blood. I was missing a significant other who cared about me, about us. I was missing a supportive boyfriend who could guide me through this process or at least acknowledge that we existed. I was missing Justin, and I hated myself for it.

The irony of unhealthy relationships is that you still crave and long for what is ultimately destroying who you are inside. I despised looking at those parent profiles because it was a reminder of the relationship that I could neither save nor fix. At that moment, I didn't hate Justin, and yet I had every reason to. After two years of sharing myself with him, he just walked away. He walked away not only from me, as he had done multiple times before, but walked away from our baby, as if she were nothing to him. The idea that I wasn't good enough for him was heartbreaking. The idea that we, she and I together, were not enough was devastating. And every profile I turned to was a reminder of how I wasn't good enough to have what they all had, a supportive partner, and a family.

Instead of pointing the finger at Justin, as I should have done, I looked inward and carried the shame of unworthiness. I replayed scenarios in my mind of how I could have been better for him. I lacked the confidence and realization that I was enough, that my baby was enough, and that Justin was the one who was inadequate. Our breakup, and his absence during my pregnancy, chained down my self-respect for years. I beat myself up time and again for not being what he needed in order to stay. I looked at the women in those profiles and wondered what they must have that I didn't. I wanted desperately to find what that was.

AFTER A LONG WORK day, I sat on the floor in my room at my brother's home, and I glanced under my bed. The four profiles I had taken home laid untouched, for weeks, on the carpet. I knew I had to make a decision and no one was going to make it for me. Ignoring those profiles was not going to make my feelings of inadequacy go away.

I began reading every profile and pondering on each one. When I reached Shawn and Alice's I noticed something different. Shawn and Alice were older than some of the couples I had looked at. They had been waiting longer, and they had no children. I was drawn to Shawn's teddy bear personality. He seemed gentle, kind, and loving.

I didn't have a list of what I wanted in the couple

who would parent my child. The thought of creating one felt superficial to me. What would the list even contain? I hope he's smart and she's pretty? There's no manual on "How to Pick the Perfect Adoptive Parents for Your Baby" and if there was one, I didn't know about it. I only knew when I had found them, I would know, and fortunately I was right. When I reached the paragraph that read: "Our decision to adopt has come easily since Alice was adopted." I grabbed the phone, called my mom, and continued reading the profile out loud: "I know how it feels to be adopted. I can anticipate the questions your child will ask and receive from peers."

"This is the one," I told my mom. "What do you think?" I could hear her holding back her emotions before she replied.

"It's perfect, and if you feel good, then I feel good about it," she confirmed.

The next day, I contacted LDS Family Services (LDSFS), the agency who would be facilitating the adoption, and told them I had found the couple that I wanted to adopt my baby girl.

"Hello. How was your week?" Ray asked.

Thus, started every Sunday phone conversation with Ray. He would call every week to see how I was holding up. He didn't back down after I told him I was firm on placing my baby girl for adoption. It didn't stop him from continuing to pursue me. I looked forward to our conversations every week and found it an escape from the harsh reality of my situation and the difficulties still ahead. After the first time Ray suggested that I marry him and that we keep the baby, we never talked about marriage again. We now had a friendship that was much more valuable than the more superficial, although still significant, relationship we had prior.

"I'm ready to move home," I announced to Ray on one of our weekly calls.

"Come home then," Ray said.

"My parents don't want me too. I think they are worried I will digress, but I miss my friends and the familiarity of home," I stated.

"Don't ask them if you can come home. Just come home," Ray said assertively.

The Arizona community and my brother's ward had accepted me and my pregnancy, or at least I felt as much. I was working two jobs and keeping myself busy and productive. I was even dating and enjoying a somewhat normal teenage life, albeit while pregnant. I admired the boys I dated. They felt no shame in being seen with me. I connected with many admirable members of my religion and with other people who were not members of the LDS church, but something was calling me home.

Facing the facts was what initially helped me begin rebuilding my confidence. My decision to place my baby for adoption, along with the strong confirmation that I received after that decision, only made my confidence grow. I was no longer shameful. I was actually proud of how much I had grown. I knew there was beauty in my consequences, and no one was going to derail me from a path that I now knew was the right path for me and for my child.

I packed up Red, once again, and told my parents I was moving home.

A SEEMINGLY UNFILLABLE HEART

Journal Entry — August 17, 2000

5:30 a.m.

My alarm goes off. I roll my ridiculously large body out of my bed. My eyes are tired and unresponsive. I am six months pregnant and can hardly sleep. The lack of rest and the anticipation of this day had me in a trance. Instead I would like to climb back into the comfort of my sheets and miss my flight altogether. I'm tired and confused about how I am supposed to feel on this day.

7:23 a.m.

I'm boarding a flight to Phoenix, AZ (I just returned home two months prior). My mother is accompanying me. We have a 10 am meeting with LDSFS and the adoptive parents, Shawn and Alice, who will be adopting my baby girl. This meeting is what LDSFS calls a "face to face". The "face to face" is a chance for the birth parents and adoptive parents to get to know each other. This meeting is only an hour long. As I'm stepping on the plane, I'm thinking to myself, *I need weeks with these people, not an hour.* There is a mixed cocktail of nervousness, excitement, and hesitation.

10:00 a.m.

I am sitting across from the adoptive couple who will be raising my baby girl. The mom is tall, thin, and beautiful. The dad is tall as well, 6'2". I am drawn to the father figure he will be in my baby's life. I'm intrigued by their loving relationship. The way he pauses and allows her to speak, before he does. They greeted me with a bouquet of stargazers, a memory box, and a journal. The quote on the outside of the journal reads, *"What is done in love is never lost."* I am guarded and nervous at first, but as the meeting proceeds, I relax. I find myself laughing and conversing as if we were long lost friends. They tell me they will name my baby, Lucy, and I feel satisfied with their choice. The connection is there, and I feel my anxiousness ease. My mother and I leave feeling positive.

We have lunch with my social worker and rehash the hour and a half meeting with her. I feel blessed and happy with where I am. I went to bed with a sense of peace and calmness. I am on the right path, and I can feel it. Thank you, God, for this precious angel that I am allowed to bring into this world. I love my decision.

FOUR

My Little Butterfly

"Everything has changed and yet, I am more me than I've ever been."-Iain Thomas

"You'll never be able to take this decision back," he stated as he slid by me in the halls of my parent's church building.

I froze, looking behind me in the direction he was walking. He turned in time to see my shock but didn't skip a beat. He held a respectable status in our ward and had a family everyone knew. Apparently, he also knew everything he needed to know about my situation. I had never had a discussion with him before receiving this unsolicited advice, but something about it hit me to the core.

How dare he walk by, drop his opinion, and continue walking, with no explanation? I was in a place of contentment. When I met Shawn and Alice, I felt peace. I had even thanked God for this place I now stood in. This gentleman's words, though, echoed around the halls. Every person I passed thereafter, I passed hesitantly, as if they had heard him, as if they agreed with him. *Did they? Was he the mouth piece for many?*

His words played on repeat in my mind for years, during delivery, during placement, post-placement, and on too many occasions after. The arrogant look on his face tainted my peaceful thoughts. I wanted to prove him wrong. I wanted to prove all of them wrong by showing them what an admirable thing I was doing. I wanted to shove happy pictures of her in his face, happy pictures of me in his face until he agreed it was the "right" thing to do. But shamelessly, on that Sunday afternoon, a part of me was afraid he was right.

I BEGAN HAVING CONTRACTIONS at 6:00 p.m. on October 4, 2000. I spread my arms from one side of the shower to the other and winced in pain. These contractions were nothing like the Braxton Hicks I had experienced before. The tug and pull of my uterus dropped me to my knees.

We arrived at the hospital around 7:00 p.m. I was dilated to a three and a half, and my contractions were now three minutes apart. My mother, my two sisters, and my best friend were all in the room with me. We watched the Country Music Awards to pass

A SEEMINGLY UNFILLABLE HEART

the time, and by 11:00 p.m., I was dilated to a five.

My emotions bounced from pure excitement to paralyzing angst, angst about what delivery would entail, but even greater concern over the tasks following delivery that I had spent the last nine months preparing for. *Am I ready, will I ever be ready? Is any girl ever prepared to become a mother? Is it the situation I find myself in that has brought such doubt or is this how every new mommy feels?* I wasn't sure.

At 12:06 a.m., I was dilated to a nine and a half Time to push. In the mix of sweat, white knuckles, and tears stemming from webs deep within me, I delivered the most beautiful baby girl. And in a moment that should have brought cheers of delight, I heard nothing but silence and felt heaviness from everyone present. This moment mirrored every step that has come previously, with its contrasting emotions and wondering whether we should rejoice or mourn.

Lucy was taken out of the room as I laid sobbing on the delivery table. *Did they take her because they know I am placing her for adoption? Will they not let me hold her?* The throbbing pain from my episiotomy demanded the attention of everyone in the room. I could hear myself whaling uncontrollably but couldn't decipher if it was the physical pain or the emotional agony of my reality. In any case, I couldn't stop myself. The flood gates had been opened, and I could no longer keep my feelings at bay. Every emotion crawled across my skin like millions of biting ants. Nothing about this felt normal. Every time I opened my mouth I could feel those pesky ants crawling back into my throat and inside of me. I had no control and no restraint. Despite the hospital gown, I was naked and vulnerable in every possible way.

After the doctor came back in to check my episiotomy, the pain subsided and so did my unbalanced emotions. I was moved into a recovery room, where my mother sat in the chair next to me, holding my hand.

Lucy was never placed in my arms after delivery because of the complications with her and with me. "Mom? I haven't even held her," I anxiously announced.

"Okay, let's see what we can do." She came back into the room with a wheel chair. "Let's go."

We made the short jaunt to the hospital nursery where a handful of newborns were sleeping. The nurse untangled the chords around my precious baby girl and placed her in my arms. She was perfect.

This is not your baby.
This is not your baby.
I heard it so clearly.

"I know," I replied into thin air, as I wrapped my arms around her innocent little body. She was angelic lying in my arms. Her innocence and complete oblivion to the reality into which she had arrived was ironic and devastating to me. Here she was, perfect in every way, and here I was feeling completely inadequate. Her life was beginning and my life, as I knew it, was ending. This was a new and beautiful beginning for her, and for me, it was a terrifying goodbye to my innocence.

This is not your baby.

What mother, before she can even take a breath,

hears those five words as she holds her newborn flesh and blood? No adoption agency, no social worker, no other birth mom had prepared me enough. Not one of them explained what it would feel like, what I might hear, or how I should feel. But how could they? Was there a way to prepare for this? The natural, motherly, instinct to tighten my grip and never let her go battled inside me as I silently, but firmly replied to the voice in my head. *I know. I know. I know she's not my baby.* I was defeated.

We left the nursery, without her. My mother pushed me in the wheelchair as we circled the hallway. I dragged my fingertips across the white walls of the hospital. There was a 1" trim lining the entire hallway. I fixated on that trim, running one finger across the top and the other across the bottom. I was analyzing so carefully, I could have aced a quiz on its details. I had a feeling that if I gave way to my actual thoughts, I'd lose my cool. It was as if that trim was the one thing tethering me to my sanity. I didn't want to welcome the opening of the flood gates again, but I also knew I should process the clear statement I had heard while holding my baby girl. I needed somewhere to channel this energy. After we circled the hallways three or four times, my mother took me back to my room.

I pulled myself into the hospital bed, and felt compelled to write. I asked for a pen and paper and wrote her a poem titled "My Little Butterfly." Each word flew out of the tip of my pen and onto that sheet of linen with ease. I signed it, pulled the covers over my head and cried thick, hot tears into that scratchy hospital pillowcase.

My Little Butterfly

You were finally here,
My Little Butterfly.
You were placed in my arms,
And I couldn't help but cry.
You were so precious so beautiful,
I stared at you with pride.
Your hands so tiny,
Your eyes so bright.
You were finally here,
My Little Butterfly.
And I knew it would be hard
To say goodbye.
I cried for you at night.
How could I let my
Little Butterfly go?
Then I thought of the new world you will see,
Of the loving parents that will
Take care of thee,
And I felt peace.
You were finally here,
My Little Butterfly.
And no matter how hard it is,
I must say goodbye.
So open your wings,
And don't be afraid to fly.
Fly away to a new life,
Where opportunities are at every door.
And my love around every corner.
You were finally here,

A SEEMINGLY UNFILLABLE HEART

My Little Butterfly.
But quickly you left,
To live your new life.
You'll always be in my heart.
Your memory in my every thought.
Those tiny hands and bright eyes.
I will forever love you
My Little Butterfly.

FIVE

The Handoff

"Our heart always transcends us." Rainer Maria Rilke

The brisk air, the smell of fresh rain, and the scenery of fall in Utah surrounded me as I carried my baby into my parent's home. My baby—the sound of it rolled off of my tongue and felt surprisingly comfortable and satisfying.

I folded myself around her like an oversized Christmas sweater. She brought me love in its purest form. I reclined into the comfort of my parent's violet Lazy Boy and slipped into a perfect state of contentment. The warmth of her body across my chest, her soft breath against the crease of my neck, the smell of Johnson & Johnson baby lotion dancing in the air, it all screamed home. I was home. She was my home. I had taken on the title of her birth mother since my final decision to place her for adoption, but at this moment, I was not her birth mother. I was her mother.

Regardless of my age, circumstances, choices, or what the future held for either of us, I was her mother. I didn't need confirmation from anyone else. She was the purest and most divine parts of me. What flowed through her veins flowed through mine, regardless of my decision, and that could not be taken from either of us.

My parent's home began to fill with friends and family who were all eager to see and hold Lucy. No amount of pictures was enough to capture a baby who you feared at some point, you'd never get to photograph again. I sat in the violet recliner, silently disturbed, and I watched as every single person doted on her. The bitter taste in my mouth didn't come from what I knew I had to do next. It came from the grim reality that my decision — the decision that I felt so alone while making — affected every person in that room. I saw agony in each of their eyes as they held her, and I realized that I was not alone in this. In fact, maybe I never was.

In that moment, I felt the universal pain I was causing every person who knew her and who knew me. I wanted to crumble inside of myself. How could I do this to everyone? How did I feel so confident in my choice and yet so blind as to how it would affect us all? I closed my eyes and drowned in the thought. *I don't think I can do this.*

My parents saw this coming. They were not convinced I would follow through with placement. My father thought it possible that once I saw Lucy, I wouldn't want to let her go. He was unsure if the bond between mother and daughter would overcome my carefully-laid plans. In fact, he was uncertain up to the minute I let her go, and he constantly reminded me that this decision was my own to make. My mother, on the other hand, seemed to believe in my plan to go through with placement, relying both on her faith and my certainty. She had a clear idea of what was the "right" thing to do and what, in the alternative, would be stemming from selfishness.

SLEEP DID NOT FIND me that Sunday evening, but motherhood did. I fed Lucy, changed her, and held her all night. For the first time, at the young age of twenty, I understood the precious gift of time. When the sun peaked through the living room window I felt my body ground itself to the earth below, and my soul lift up above reality. I no longer felt connected to my physical body. My movements and actions were on autopilot. I called my social worker and let her know I was ready for placement at 1 p.m.

"Be a good girl. Remember how much I love you. Remember my voice. Be a good girl," I whispered, into the tiniest ear I had ever seen.

My feet hung an inch above the floor, as I sank into the faux leather, maroon couch. The pale-yellow walls and the fake, dust-collecting tree in the corner were not new to me. I sat in this room many times before. I met my social worker in this room weekly. I was told that Justin, Lucy's birth father, had signed his rights away in this room. I signed my rights way in this room. I signed away my rights to the baby I now held in my arms.

But right now, this room felt foreign to me. It felt smaller. Today I didn't recognize anything familiar in this room, but saw only my twenty-year-old self and a tiny baby girl I had given birth to four days prior. This was the last time I'd see her ears that tiny, her delicate hand wrapped around my finger in that way. It was the last time I'd know her as my own. I'd been dreading this moment for nine months, and yet it was here. It was time to say goodbye.

"You are my little butterfly. You have many great and beautiful things ahead of you. Please, please come find me someday. I love you. Be a good girl," I pleaded, as my tears soaked the pale pink blanket she was swaddled in. I heard a faint knock on the door and in walked my social worker.

"Are you ready?" she politely asked. "Shawn is here. He is ready when you are." Shawn had made the trip from Arizona to Utah alone.

WHEN I FIRST PICKED Shawn and Alice, Alice was pregnant. They didn't relay this to LDSFS because doing so would have taken them off of the list of waiting couples. Alice had miscarried many times before this pregnancy, and they were fearful she would lose this child, too, and lose their spot on the adoption waiting list. Finally, they had to come clean, and a few months after I picked them, I got a phone call from my social worker explaining the situation. Alice was due six weeks after me with a boy, and now I had the choice to pick someone else if I wanted.

I made a quick call to a friend and explained what was going on. His response reassured me that Alice's pregnancy made no difference in my confirmation to place my baby with this particular couple. I agreed. If anything, this made it all the more exciting to think Lucy would have a sibling so close to her age. I moved forward with Shawn and Alice, knowing they would be welcoming twins, a boy and a girl!

Alice was not present for what LDSFS calls "the handoff." The handoff is when you, as a birth mother, place your baby in the arms of the adoptive couple. Your other option is to place your baby in your social worker's arms, and he or she takes the baby to the adoptive couple. I never hesitated in deciding between my options. It should be me who hands my baby to the couple who will carry the responsibility of raising her. This was my gift to give. I had been called to do this, and I wanted to be present for the final moment of saying goodbye.

Alice was seven and half months pregnant at the time of the handoff, and because her pregnancy was considered high risk, the doctors would not let her travel to Utah for the handoff. It was disappointing not to see her again, but I knew it was important for her to stay healthy and care for her unborn child.

"Send him in," I replied to my social worker. "I'm ready."

Journal Entry — October 9, 2000

I said goodbye today to my little butterfly. We all met at LDSFS at 1 p.m. It took about one hour to sign all of the paperwork. When I asked my social worker for the time to record on the papers, she answered with 1:35 p.m. I smiled and thought, *Lucy was born at 1:35 a.m.* After the paperwork was completed, my mom and dad came in to say their goodbyes. Then I was given time alone with her. I told her how much I love her and how hard this is. I told her to be a good girl and to come find me someday. I kissed her on the forehead and told my social worker I was ready.

Shawn entered the room. His chin was quivering as he walked in. He asked me how I was feeling. He sat down next to me, and I slowly handed Lucy to him. He cried and smiled.

"What a beautiful baby," he said.

He couldn't stop looking at her and neither could I. We talked about Alice and how she was feeling, and then my parents came in. My dad was heavy-hearted. He cried, and I cried, and my mom cried, and then my social worker started to cry. It was a bittersweet moment for all of us. But I know I made the right decision. I know Lucy is where she needs to be, and she is happy.

I miss her more than anything in the world. I cried all night. I miss her so much already! I kept picturing her cute little feet, toes, and hands. She is such a beautiful baby. Today was a hard day. This is the hardest day of my whole life. I pray for strength to get through this. I am weak, and I miss her every minute, but I try to stay positive. I try not to get depressed and keep my head up. I want to become a better person for her. I want her to be proud of me. I want her to be proud to say I am her birth mom. I love her so much!

I love you Lucy. I will think of you always and miss you every minute.

I CLIMBED INTO THE back seat of my parent's Ford Explorer. There was a silent reverence. The greatest gift had been given, and though it was a powerful and positive experience, the gloom and exhaustion hung heavy in the air. We began the 10-minute drive home. I sat next to Lucy's empty car seat, its hollowness mirroring the emptiness I felt inside. It had been only hours before when she was sleeping peacefully next to me, and now she was gone. I couldn't stop looking at her car seat. If I stared at it long enough, would she reappear in her proper place next to me? Somewhere I believed she would. I was fixated on this fantasy. We arrived at my parent's house, and I threw myself onto their plush sheets in their king size bed and stayed there the rest of the day and thru the night.

The hole inside of me where Lucy should be, swirled in my chest as the night went on. It twirled around in a circular motion taking more and more of me as it spun until it felt like it had taken all of me. No part of me felt whole. In fact, I could no longer even find myself in this space of despair. I had nothing more to give, nothing more anyone could take. There was no thought of how I would carry on or what comes next because there was no part of me to carry on. Someone could take their hands, place them around my neck and squeeze, leaving my limp body sprawled out on those plush sheets, and I would feel exactly the same as I did before that experience. I felt no desire for anything — no thirst, no hunger — I was completely void.

"No! Don't take her," I screamed out. "No!"

I woke up in a pool of sweat and full of frenzy, still in my parents' bed. I had just reached the point of unconsciousness when the nightmare took over. Someone was running out the door with Lucy, and no matter what I did, I could never reach her. That first nightmare was only the beginning of what continued sporadically for years after placement. Surviving the first night without Lucy has continued to be one of the most challenging experiences of my life.

Journal Entry — October 28, 2000

Dear Lucy,

This letter is the most important letter I will ever write, and I pray you will feel my incredible love for you. When I found out I was pregnant, I was scared. I wasn't married and struggling with my self-esteem. Your birth father and I decided marriage was not the best choice. I started thinking about adoption. I wanted what was best for you, what would give you the future you deserved.

A SEEMINGLY UNFILLABLE HEART

Many countless hours were spent praying and crying. I was left on my own to make the right decision. I knew I could take care of you, but every reason I had for keeping you felt like selfish reasons to me. I had to think about you and how your life would be without a father figure.

I received an obvious answer to place you for adoption. I'll never forget the day I read your parents' profile. I had a strong confirmation they would be your parents. I called and read the profile to my mother, and she cried. She knew, as well as I, Shawn and Alice were the ones.

My pregnancy went by quickly, and I enjoyed every day I had with you in my tummy. You would always get the hiccups and kick me at night. Your delivery was the best day of my life! You were my little butterfly, I was anxious to see. You were a beautiful baby. Everyone thought so. Everyone loves you! They all came to see you, to say goodbye, and to tell you how much they love you.

The night before I placed you for adoption, I didn't sleep one minute. I didn't want to miss one thing. I wanted to stay in the moment forever. You were peaceful as you slept. I sang to you, read you my poem, and cuddled with you. I knew this was my last night with you. I cried all night.

The day I placed you for adoption was unbearable. My body ached everywhere. I started the day with a long, strong prayer. I asked for strength to do what I knew you deserved. I believed I was doing what would make you the happiest. It was a bittersweet moment when I put you in Shawn's arms. I couldn't stop staring at you. You were so beautiful, and I was proud of you.

Shawn left with you, and my tears flowed freely. It was hard to see you go. The first night without you was agony, but I knew I was doing the right thing. I only hope you understand my decision. It wasn't easy, and there hasn't been one easy day without you. I have to find strength, every morning and night, to get out of bed and live a life you can be proud of.

Lucy, I love you so much. Please, never think I just gave you away because I didn't love you. You have many people who love you. Your memory is always with me, wherever I go. You're my little butterfly. Your future is full of good things. Be happy, be positive, and know you have a guardian angel who is always thinking of you.

I am confident in my decision to place you for adoption, but that doesn't mean the days are easy without you. I struggle each day, but I know you are happy. Shawn and Alice are an answer to my prayers. They are the most amazing people I have ever met. Their smiles glow with love and kindness. You are blessed to have them as your parents.

Please Lucy, I hope you know I am sorry for putting you in this situation. You're an angel, sweetheart. Don't ever be afraid to open your wings and fly.

XOXO, your birth mom

SIX

Birth Mother Baskets

"Those who bring sunshine to the lives of others cannot keep it from themselves." -James Matthew Barrie

The fresh breeze brought life back to my face. My permanently swollen eyes, still bloodshot from the week before, squinted at the bright sun. My parents' backyard was full of russet-colored quakies, their warmth resting on the burgundy deck bench I was sitting on. Flappy, stretch-marked skin dangled over the front of my sweat pants. A dark hue lined my body, from my pelvis to my mid-section. My breast full of unused breast milk stained my bra. My droopy, empty stomach was the only ironic keepsake I had of Lucy. I could no longer recognize my own body, but somehow I slipped into my mother skin with the ease of changing my shirt.

Often, I would overhear my parents' sympathetic whispers of concern. They were uncertain about how to react to my grief-stricken behavior, tiptoeing around me like a sleeping newborn. They feared one wrong move or sudden noise would rattle the sliver of sanity I faked having. The week after Lucy's birth was a constant revolving door of voiceless inner howling and dazed irrational thoughts. Time ceased to exist. The day absorbed the night. The night absorbed the day. It made no difference to me. Somewhere in my subconscious, I was building a lighthouse, a beacon toward Lucy. I naturally called out to her, and her absence dragged behind me like weights tied to my feet. My soul knew a piece of me was missing.

I DIDN'T HEAR THE knock at the door or the conversation taking place in the next room over. The pull of the sliding glass door turned my head. Ray was standing in the opening.

"How are you feeling?" he asked, as he sat next to me on the bench.

With no reply, I curled my frail frame under the crease of his arm and rested my thoughts in his chest. It had been weeks since I had seen him. He left for a hunting trip the week Lucy was born, never seeing her in the hospital or at my parents' home before her placement. Ray never met Lucy.

Very few words were spoken in those moments. As I leaned against the strength of his body, I knew he would never let me go, and I knew this is where I always wanted to be. The abnormal warmth of that fall day and the way my heart easily bled into Ray's will never escape my memory.

The following four months were jam-packed with wedding preparations. It was a whirlwind of passionate new love polluted with grief and loss. My parents, as they had done before, backed my sudden decision to marry Ray. My father gave his blessing with only a hint of uneasiness. My feelings for Ray shifted immediately after Lucy's placement from a loving friend to husband and life-partner. Once I fell for Ray, I didn't look back. If everything else failed, I knew Ray never would. I was confident he would never leave me behind. He would armor up and go to battle for me and for our family. I was convinced that with Ray, my home would forever be filled with love and laughter. Ray and I married in February of 2001.

I WALKED IN TO find her hands grasped around the edges of a two-sided lined paper. She was seated behind the desk at LDSFS. I had never seen her there before. She was mesmerized by the words she was reading. She didn't notice my entrance. I was standing in front of her waiting for her acknowledgment.

"Hello," I said. "I'm here to pick up my letter. Someone called and said it was here."

During the early-2000s, communication between adoptive couples and birth parents went through the adoption agency first. The agency would call the birth parent to let them know they had a letter ready to be picked up. Every time I picked up a letter, the envelope was already torn open. My social worker read every word before I was allowed to see it. So why would someone other than my social worker be sitting here reading my letter? The woman looked up and saw me standing right in front of her.

"Oh, hello Gina," she replied.

How does she know my name? I thought.

"I have your letter right here," she said, as she folded up the letter in her hands and placed it into the envelope while gathering the handful of photos scattered across her desk. She smiled and handed the envelope to me.

I was stunned at her nonchalant manner, acting as though it were completely normal for her to be reading through my life like it was entertainment. All of the sudden, I caught a glimpse into how communication between the adoptive couple, birth parent, and agency was seriously flawed.

When you're a child, you grow up believing your parents know everything. They can fix it all, heal all wounds, fill your belly with good food, and help you with your homework. My parents were geniuses until they weren't. There is a moment for many young teenagers where they recognize this truth for the first time. Parents do their best to find solutions to problems as they go along. I felt this way after leaving the agency. I had put my trust and even my baby, in the hands of LDSFS, and when I left that day, I felt betrayed.

LDSFS didn't know what the letters meant to me. The people there don't know how difficult it is to place a baby for adoption. They make educated guesses on how to solve problems that present themselves in each moment. The receptionist wanted to dive her nose into a dramatic story. She tried to put herself in the "feel good moments" of a personal, grief-stricken, and heartbreaking story. She wanted to reap the reward of my climb to the summit without any of the work. This, however, was not just a story. This was my life!

Every birth mother has her own "triggers," or events that put her right back in the place of desperation and loneliness. This experience, for me, made me feel violated. I lost respect for an agency who I thought had my best interest in mind. It felt like as soon as I was no longer a sale they had to close, I became little more than a good story to keep them entertained. I placed my baby for adoption and the adoptive couple received what they paid for. From that point on, I was a good story to discuss over diet cokes in the office every morning.

I walked back to my car, sat in the driver seat and cried. I cried tears of wild frustration. I cried tears of hot embarrassment. My life had become a circus for people's entertainment. The employee's grimy hands had tainted the authentic message of Shawn and Alice's letter. I no longer cared about the letter I had so anxiously awaited. I wanted to rip it to shreds and toss it out the car window. It felt used and impure, and ironically, I felt the same. It took every ounce of humanity for me to not scream in her face, "This is my life! Not some soap opera for you to binge-watch." For years, I felt powerless in a situation I had absolutely no control over. The truth was, I didn't know how many people read my letters before me. I didn't know if anything LDSFS had promised me was truthful or would be backed up in times of conflict. I didn't know if Shawn and Alice were being truthful with me. It was all out of my hands.

I never forgave "what's her name" behind the desk, and I never looked at LDSFS in the same way. I never read another letter without thinking someone had already analyzed its entirety before I was even able to hold it. I started to recognize the holes in LDSFS. They were no longer the "all-knowing" parental figure in my adoption journey, and I didn't trust anything I had been told. I started thinking of ways to improve things for other birth moms.

I noticed a serious lack of birth mothers who spoke out about their experiences with placement. I needed more guidance, and I craved connection with other women who had been through this process before. Was my reaction to my letter being pre-read by a stranger normal? I didn't know. How could I know? I yearned for someone who had been in my shoes, to show me the way, to confirm that whatever emotions I was feeling were okay.

I WAS PREGNANT WITH our first child when I called Ray and said, "Babe, I think I just had an 'aha moment.'" He laughed and asked me what this grand "aha moment" was all about.

Every year around Christmas time, I would do some type of service project. My passion for service was encouraged in part by having been raised in an LDS family. The LDS church encourages service to others, and it teaches about the joy service brings to your life. I spent a lot of my youth serving those around me, and I am grateful for those lessons and the way they established in me a love for humanitarian work.

This particular Christmas I wanted to do something for my fellow birth mothers. As I was driving down Main Street in my hometown, a question came to me: What if birth moms didn't have to leave the hospital empty-handed? What if they could go home with something just for them, a gift of some kind, instead of diaper and formula samples that just reinforce their loss?

"I want to put together gift baskets for birth moms. Baskets full of items just for them. Not baby stuff," I excitedly announced to Ray. "I'll ask for donations from local businesses, and we'll deliver them to hospitals and adoption agencies."

"Sounds like a great idea," he agreed as he did so many times before, without knowing what he was getting himself into.

I started my search the next day, surrounding myself with phone books on the floor of our quaint three-bedroom condo. I was on a mission. I was looking for items suited for a birth mother, post-delivery and placement. I wanted bath salts, lotions, blankets, and journals. Anything to help her feel pampered and appreciated. I had no idea how people would react to my new service project, but something deep inside felt compelled to do this. My goal was to fill twenty baskets by Christmas.

I called every local business that carried the particular items I was looking for. During the first few hours, I heard a lot of rejections, but that didn't stop me. It only made me dial faster. I knew this was a good idea, and I just needed to find the right people. After a few days of reaching out, I spent the following week driving around, picking up donated items, and filling our spare third bedroom with baskets, tissue paper, and anything else I could use. With each donation, my confidence grew. My goal of twenty baskets quickly turned into forty baskets by Christmas.

As I began assembling baskets, I thought about each item and what was appropriate to give. Each basket contained a letter from me, letting each birth mother know that she was not alone. I too had felt similar emotions. Each basket also contained the poem I had written for Lucy, "My Little Butterfly." I delivered these first baskets to LDSFS and a local hospital, and the baskets were welcomed with open arms. I hoped every birth mother who received a basket would feel loved. The vision I had of watching them leave the hospital or agency with a basket full of items just for them made my heart soar. I wasn't trying to replace their babies—I knew nothing could ever do that—I was merely reaching out a hand to say, *You are not alone in your journey, and this basket is all about you!*

As the New Year began, I started receiving donations from companies that were unable to donate before Christmas. Those first one hundred "no's" I received turned into "yeses." I continued picking up donations every month and realized my Christmas service project didn't have to be limited to Christmas; I could deliver baskets all year round. When I received enough donations to fill ten baskets,

I would donate them, and start over again. This was the beginning of Birth Mother Baskets (BMB).

"This letter is addressed to you," Ray stated as he tossed the rectangular envelope my way.

I didn't recognize the return name or address. I slid open the edges, and a check fell onto the table. I flipped it over to see $100.00 made out to Birth Mother Baskets. The check was from a lady who lived near us. She had seen my picture and request for donations in our local newspaper. Her check were the largest I had received. I turned to Ray with tears in my eyes, "It's a check for $100.00 for the baskets."

I could hardly believe what I was saying. The vast amount of gratitude, the confirmation that I was doing something important, the pat on the back, it all hit me with a wave of appreciation. I sat at our oak dining table and stared at the check for another half hour. Someone, a stranger, sent this to me. This stranger has faith in me, has faith in my idea. This stranger believes in what I'm doing. I felt accomplished. Those ten thousand pennies carried me for the next fourteen years of serving and developing Birth Mother Baskets, a non-profit organization. No other donation felt as significant as the first one, and yet they were all welcomed and appreciated. I continually return to those feelings of the first confirmation that I was doing something right, something beautiful.

I was proud of my decision to place Lucy for adoption. I had no shame in this choice. Her placement allowed me to rip off the scarlet letter that had been figuratively sewn onto me during pregnancy, and to reject the judgmental comments that came along with it. There was no need to carry them any further. I placed a beautiful baby girl with a family, and there was no shame in something I felt so much pride in. I often thought about birth mothers who had placed decades before me, most of them sent away to maternity wards away from the comfort and familiarity of home. The secrecy surrounding adoption and birth mothers infuriated me. I cried for the women who had their babies taken from them, with no choice. I ached for their grief and was grateful for the time and space in which I placed.

I felt drawn to share my story because there were so few birth mothers who were doing so. I felt a calling to speak up, and I knew I needed to be a voice for those who feared judgment. The first donation and the positive reaction I had received for BMB, gave me the extra push to be brave in what I felt compelled to do. I call myself "brave" a bit hesitantly because I recognize how privileged I was to have a strong foundation of support and love, which made it easier for me to stand up.

I became an adoption advocate. This role entailed speaking at adoption agency meet-ups, sitting on birth parent panels, attending adoption conferences, and guiding adoptive couples. Every event or fundraiser led back to BMB and the need to fill baskets with pampering items for birth mothers.

I became Gina, the birth mom. I was an expert in the field because of my personal experience. I had felt those thorns of grief. I had been judged. I had given a piece of my heart to a couple I hardly knew, leaving a hole that would never be filled. I had found myself on the floor begging for relief. And then, quite unexpectedly, I had found purpose in educating people on what a birth mother sounds like, looks like, and what she feels. This was who I was now, and I was proud of myself. There were few times in my life when I felt proud with such confidence. In the thick of running Birth Mothers Baskets, I felt pride.

In the midst of filling baskets and speaking out, I felt connected to Lucy. By staying close to the adoption community, it seemed like I could feel her near me. The drive to grow BMB stemmed from a desire to make Lucy proud of me and proud of the work I had done. I didn't want her to be embarrassed by me or to hesitate to tell people I was her birth mother.

That drive and purpose guided me to accomplish great things in my life. Every delivered birth mother basket, over a thousand by the time I stopped donating, was given with the intent of giving something to Lucy. I was able to comfort my fellow birth mothers and leave a traceable line of unconditional love and, in a way, proof that Lucy was not forgotten.

BMB created new opportunities I would not have had otherwise, including being a Teen Pregnancy Ambassador for "Power in You," a program started by Mary Kay Huntsman, former First Lady of Utah. Power in You helps children and teenagers deal with the emotional side of adversity through peer-to-peer and grownup support, and it was a pleasure to be involved.

I was also invited to the Utah Governors' Mansion for a luncheon with fellow ambassadors. Walking the prestigious hallways, I allowed the significance of the moment to sink in. I was in the Governors' Mansion, as a guest! My chest was full of pride and gratitude. The steps getting to this point had been strenuous. In fact, each step was an act of survival, and attempt to simply get through the next day, or even the next hour, as I waded through my grief. In retrospect, however, each step was leading me to opportunities such as this, to the steps to the Governors' Mansion.

Throughout the years I found creative ways to earn money for BMB. Every cent went back to filling and delivering baskets. One year, I came up with something that I called "Word Birds," a craft-project I made with ceramic birds from the Dollar Tree store. I hand-painted each one with a word such as *gratitude, strength, courage* or *love*. I sold each Word Bird for $10, profiting $9 from of each one. The money I received here and there kept baskets shipping at a regular pace for a few months. It also helped that I was a skilled bargain shopper, finding high quality items at the lowest price possible, in order to fill baskets to the rim.

Thanks to a connection with a friend at our local Harley Davidson shop, I started hosting a yearly BMB auction there. Each auction brought in enough money to ship at least a basket or two per month for a year. Although it was a constant battle to come up with new and creative ways to fund BMB, I figured delivering one basket a month was better than no basket at all. In addition, I was able to fulfill every basket request that came in, plus donate to agencies and hospitals. If I didn't have the money, I pulled from our savings, making sure every birth mother could leave the hospital with a basket.

Journal Entry — October 9, 2009

Dear Lucy,
Today I started the Birth Mother Baskets blog. I've wanted to do this for some time now, and after having lunch with a friend, I felt like now was a good time to start. I started BMB almost six years ago. I called around to local businesses asking for donations to fill gift baskets, and I donated them to local hospitals and adoption agencies. We have filled over three hundred baskets so far, and I'm hoping with donations coming from the blog, we will be able to fill even more.

The baskets are filled with pampering items for a birth mom such as candles, jewelry, books, a small blanket, journal, make-up, and gift certificates. Every basket has a copy of the poem I wrote you in the hospital, "My Little Butterfly." It is typically framed and on decorative paper. I've spent a lot of time speaking about our adoption story. I do a lot of gatherings where I supply the baskets, and people donate items to go inside of them. I share my story with the group, and we assemble baskets. I love doing this project. It helps me heal and is a great way of honoring you! I get to show off your picture and tell people all about you.

I hope BMB carries on for many more years to

come. Thank you for picking me to bring you into this world. I am blessed to be your birth mother. I love you!

XOXO, your birth mom

Journal Entry — November 6, 2009

Dear Lucy,

The Birth Mother Basket blog has been a huge success! Two days ago, I sent a basket to a birth mom in Rexburg, Idaho. She is due any day now. When I ship baskets I typically send them in a cute bag instead of a basket, since it's much easier to ship. I talked to my neighbor today, and her cousin is placing her baby for adoption on Thanksgiving weekend. I'm going to put together a basket for her tomorrow. I have given three hundred and seventeen baskets since I started. My heart is full! I love serving these young women who are starting on this adventure of adoption. My heart goes out to them in these first trying months of high emotions and questions.

I feel closer to you as I deliver baskets. It brings a whole new purpose to my decision to place. It keeps you close to me in a way most would not understand. I also sold my second painting a few days ago. I was excited to do so. The Universe is excellent—you do good for others, and good will come your way. I truly believe this! My life is being blessed in many ways as I'm serving those around me. I'm happy, hopeful, and loving you!

A SEEMINGLY UNFILLABLE HEART

XOXO, your birth mom
Journal Entry — February 13, 2010

Dear Lucy,

I met Ashley today. She is a birth mother of twenty years now. She found the Birth Mother Basket blog from a friends' blog and contacted me about getting involved. Ashley placed when she was sixteen years old, and last year had the opportunity to meet her son. We have been talking for a few weeks now, and it was great to get to meet her face to face.

Ashley has found a corporate lawyer who is going to help us start a non-profit organization for the baskets, and he's doing it for free! I am ecstatic and feel like I've been working towards this for six years. I can't believe I am months away from my dream. I will be the President of Birth Mother Baskets, a non-profit organization, and Ashley will be the Vice President. The sky is the limit here. I can't wait to see how much more we will be able to do. We will have more donations, and more baskets will be going out, not only in Utah but nationwide. I am thrilled and feeling blessed.

XOXO, your birth mom

Birth Mother Basket Tracking
(Not all basket deliveries from December 2006-November 2010 are listed here.)

December 2006
- 20 baskets delivered to LDSFS and two hospitals.

June 2009
- 14 baskets delivered to one adoption agency.

October 2009
- One basket dropped off at my mom's house, to give to a friend's daughter.

November 2009
- One basket delivered to a birth mother in Idaho. Due November 20th.

February 2010
- One basket sent to a birth mother living in a shelter home in Idaho.
- Three baskets delivered to LDSFS.

March 2009
- One basket delivered to my mom's friend at work.
- Two baskets sent to family friends.

November 2010
- 12 baskets delivered to LDSFS.
- One basket sent to a friend of a friend.
- One basket for Ashley's church member.

A SEEMINGLY UNFILLABLE HEART

Letters and emails received that touched my heart, just a few of many.

I can't express in words the happiness your sweet basket brought to our little friend. Thank you so much for your time and effort. What a great service! It is sweet people like you that make these times easier.

I received one of your Birth Mother Baskets, and I am deeply grateful. I feel very special to have received such a gift from someone I don't know anyone who has gone through a similar situation. I am very grateful for you, and thank you so much for the basket. I love it!

I think what you are doing is amazing! My neighbor told me about your website last night. We are in the process of adopting a little boy. It would be amazing if you could send our birth mother a basket. I believe in what you are doing so much. We plan to give her a gift as well, but I think it would be special to have someone she doesn't know give her a basket.

Thank you for your beautiful story. As a child of adoption I always hoped for that reunion and knowledge that my birth parents longed for me too. Sadly, I never got that from my birth mother before she died. A connection is made through pregnancy and birth that adoption doesn't erase. Yes, I have great parents and I am lucky to have been adopted, but that hole will remain. Reading your story allowed me to see a birth mother's experience and think maybe my mother thought of me too. Thank you!

SEVEN

Dear, Grief

"Feel what you need to feel and then let it go. Do not let it consume you." -Dhiman

"*No!* No! Don't take him!"

I sat straight up and reached over for Ray, waking him dramatically. "Someone is in the house. I know it."

"You're okay. No one is in the house." As many times, as I had awakened him over this recurring nightmare, Ray was always so thoughtful and concerned.

"Do you want me to check the house?" he would ask.

"Yes, please."

He'd spend the next 10 minutes opening every closet door, looking under the beds and unlocking and relocking the front door. He would come back to bed and confirm everything was okay.

When the nightmares first started, someone was always taking Lucy from me. After giving birth to my son, Jack, my subconscious made a switch, and someone was always taking him. In retrospect, I was experiencing an automatic, natural response to placing Lucy for adoption, but it was much more intense and physiological than anyone could have prepared me for. My body's reaction to her absence was rooted in the fear that I would never be allowed to keep a baby of my own. I was aware that these thoughts, nightmares, and reactions were most likely abnormal, but I had nothing to compare them to.

My anxiety reached an all-time high when my son, Jack, became ill and had to spend an evening in the hospital. When we first arrived, Jack began painfully crying, and neither Ray nor I could soothe him. When the nurse came in to assist, I walked out of the room in frustration. I leaned my back against the wall in the hallway, sunk to the ground, and cried out in begging sobs.

"Please don't take him from me," I pleaded with God, The Universe, and the negative force that had it out for me. "I can't do this again. I can't say goodbye to another baby. Please heal him!"

Jack was not in a life or death situation but in my head, he was. He would be taken from me. All of the nightmares led up to this very moment. He would die, and Ray and I would be left grieving once again.

Fortunately, this was not actually happening, but my heart and soul believed it so sincerely.

Over time the nightmares decreased, and my nights filled with tearful grief and suffering disappeared. As time went on, I began to forget about the long nights when I had kept Ray up smearing his white under shirt with my mascara. He had to remind me, a decade later, how difficult those first few months were. The nightmares, on the other hand, I never forgot. They found their way back into my life years later, and the grief always returned, without exception.

Journal Entry – August 10, 2017

Dear Grief,

My fair weathered friend, except you don't only come around when things are difficult. Your vile face creeps itself into my life when I least expect it. Showing no signs of mercy or forgiveness. You don't care if I'm in the middle of grocery shopping or taking the kids to school. You ooze your heavy, tar-like webs into my every thought and force me into what feels like walking in quicksand. Your strength and resilience are beyond anything I have ever experienced or witnessed before. No amount of meditation, sacred gemstones, or rituals will loosen your grip. Like a true fighter, you change your behavior depending on your victim's knowledge. Once I figure out how to block your right punch, you hit me with a left uppercut. The force of your blow drops me to my knees screaming out for mercy from your power.

The irony about every passing year is that I

actually believe one of these days I will finally knock you out, win the battle, and I'll raise my arm in victory. For seventeen years you have dragged me to the mat to meet head to head. For seventeen years you have shown no pity for my lack of ability to beat you. Your maniacal laugh vibrates around my suffering. You call upon me unexpectedly and throw the first unofficial, illegal, punch before I even recognize I have entered the ring. I despise you! I loathe everything you stand for, taking victims at your leisure. The zealous way you float around this world, sucking in helpless souls as if they belong to you.

Over time, I have grown stronger and smarter. Show your filthy face! I know you will without permission. Knock on my door! I'm waiting for you. After all of this time, I know this fight will be different. I have spent enough time in the ring with you to know your energy will die out. You'll get bored. You'll get distracted. You'll swoosh away to latch on to someone new. If I can sit still for a moment, if I cannot react so quickly to your first hit, I will wear you out. If I acknowledge your presence with grace, if I recognize your visit is never forever then I won't panic and drop to my knees. Yes, you'll come in with your rage, your power, your strength, and I will stare straight into your bloodshot eyes and say through tears of strength, "I am not afraid of you anymore."

After many battles, the losing streak is over. I am the champion now! I choose how to react to your strike. I decide to sit with you in the ring because the only thing constant about your visits is that you will come again. The less I combat you, the quicker you will leave, and I will conquer. Move along but be prepared. My voice will not be silent. I will teach others that they, too, have the power to beat you. No one is weaker than your inability to endure. Your short attention span only gets more pitiful when your victim accepts and acknowledges your presence. I will teach this skill, my fair-weather friend, Grief. Because I know by doing so, you will spend fewer days in my world and more time searching for the weak. You won't find the weak here.

I developed a method for dealing with the flood of Grief showing his face. I'd repeat to myself, *Hello, Grief. I see you. I hear you. I acknowledge you are here today. I do not welcome you, but I will not be ashamed of your presence. I am not afraid of you. I will only allow what is necessary to heal, but I will not dwell on my emotions. I will not allow you to take over me. The emotions and pain will pass, as you will too. Goodbye, Grief.*

Accepting Grief's presence is about allowing myself to be okay with Grief being there and withholding judgment about the frequency or strength of each visit. Accepting the fight was going to happen win, lose, or draw allowed me to accept myself win, lose or draw. Some days I did feel like the champion, not only in my battle with Grief but also in the battle with myself. We face this battle daily, with or without Grief, as we war with negative self-talk. *How many times have I found myself in the ring alone, face to face with myself?*

I wonder if some of you have found yourself

there as well. Once I learned how to tolerate the fight with Grief, I saw myself winning more battles with myself. I started to pay attention to my reactions and gained control of my actions. Acknowledging that every one of my feelings was acceptable gave me the power to win. I began to see my tendency to judge myself, judge my emotions, and judge my weakness, which only brought more suffering. I learned to expand the conversation with Grief into a discussion with just about any negative thought I had.

Hello, Loneliness. I see you. I hear you. I acknowledge you are here today. I do not welcome you, but I will not be ashamed of your presence. I am not afraid of you. I will only allow what is necessary to heal, but I will not dwell on my emotions. I will not allow you to take over me. The emotions and pain will pass, as you will too. Goodbye Loneliness.

Accepting negative emotions wasn't the only helpful skill I acquired along this path. Journaling has played a significant role in allowing and accepting feelings, and then ultimately releasing them. Writing letters to Lucy helped me feel like we were still having a conversation. I could jump into my journal and tell her about my day, as if she were listening to me. I shared the bliss, and I shared the ugly, but most importantly, I shared. I would journal the feelings giving them a resting place. That resting place was not sitting heavy on my heart once they found a new bed in my journal.

I also learned more about meditating, which became an immensely helpful tool for my grieving and my mental state. Meditation gave me the advantage of inner stillness before getting in the ring

A SEEMINGLY UNFILLABLE HEART

with my opponents. At first, my practice seemed near impossible. To sit in silence for a measly five minutes was challenging. How does one shut off all thought, especially one who tends to over think how she tied her shoelaces this morning? Consistency was the one thing I had going for me. I refused to stop. I am stubborn that way. The few minutes I was able to master my thoughts were the few minutes where I felt the most peace.

Don't play hide and seek with Grief. Don't allow him to pull you into a deep, lonely hiding spot where you disconnect from those who are trying to find you. Shame happens to be Grief's best friend, and when the two combine, they can cause serious damage. If you see them sitting together on the bus, I don't recommend you sit next to them.

There really is no shame in living with Grief. There is no timeline or rule about when you are not allowed to cry anymore. There is no timeline for when you should or shouldn't feel other emotions, but shame would like you to think otherwise. I am permitting you to let go of how things are supposed to be and allow no restrictions when it comes to the unpredictable Grief. Don't hide away when Grief pays his visit. Shame will knock you down and make you feel weak, but there is power in numbers. Reach out to those closest to you, lean on them, share your thoughts. You need them, and they need you. Allow them to see you, with Grief on your back and Shame knocking on your door. It's okay not to be okay. Don't be ashamed of where you're at in the grieving process. Don't be ashamed of how your body is naturally reacting. Don't let Grief and Shame play together.

Some mornings, I will wake up to find Grief has been sleeping next to me, and my first thought is to pull my down covers over my head and pretend he's not there. The cold chills he sends up my spine never allow me to do so, and I know better than to ignore him. Those tar webs can spread from the tip of your toes to the crown of your head. You'll feel stuck in this moment forever, but you're not. You will endure. Take a long walk. Go for a hike. Call a friend, preferably one who doesn't mind you shedding a few tears. Meet for coffee or lunch.

You have permission to be selfish when Grief comes. Taking care of yourself is acceptable. Take a hot bath. Climb into a good book, and lose yourself in a simple, healthy pleasure. Hell, binge-watch a reality show, every season, in one sitting. It's okay! When Grief pays his visits, it's about surviving, and the exact way that you accept his visit is completely up to you. Sit in the tears, wipe the tears, be selfish and care for yourself, and then dust off your shoes and do something for someone else.

Serving others allowed me to be more accepting of Grief. Once BMB was up and running, and I found ways to give back instead of wallowing in self-pity, I felt a shift in how I presented my adoption story as a whole. There was no denying I was in pain and grieving. I was still waking up screaming in the night. But during the day I could stand in front of a crowd and be proud of my decision, proud of a decision that came with night terrors, grief, and post-traumatic stress. I didn't stand in front of a crowd of adoptive professionals, adoptive couples, and fellow birth mothers licking my wounds and begging for relief. I stood in front of them honored to be able to serve them, honored to be a voice for many who needed to hear—*it's okay to not be okay*. Grieve, scream, laugh, be angry, and then move toward good feeling and thoughts.

Serving those around me became my source of strength. It created an incredible sense of security in me that I wouldn't have found otherwise. As hard as it can be, when Grief pays his visit, look for ways to serve those around you. All humans experience despair, so if anyone can relate to a human in despair, it's another human! We have all been in a moment of need, every single one of us. Be understanding, and use your experiences to pull those around you out of their hellish storms. Be a lighthouse. Be a beacon. And as you do, you will find Grief's visits weaken.

When you find yourself standing on the victory platform with your arms in the air, a shiny gold medal around your neck, whether you've won the battle against negative self-talk or finally knocked out old Grief, celebrate! Celebrate the beauty of mastering your emotions. And when I say mastering, I mean accepting and allowing all of the feels rather than feeling shameful and running from them. This is an epic moment! Say goodbye to Grief, goodbye to loneliness, and whatever other demon you are demolishing. Celebrate yourself and your heroic wins.

"I WANT TO WALK you through a session of hypnotherapy," Jared stated.

"Okay," I hesitantly replied.

"Hypnotherapy is a complementary and alternative medicine in which the imagination is used to help with various problems, such as breaking bad habits or coping with stress," he explained

This was not my first time in therapy. I had seen rooms similar to this one when I was a teenager. Back then, I tried to do exactly what was expected so my sessions would end quickly. As an adult, I sat on the couch like a sponge. I was more than ready for this to have an impact on my life. I was accepting the advice and guidance from a much more mature point of view.

Jared started the relaxation steps toward hypnotherapy. He asked me to visualize a staircase. The staircase in my mind was familiar to me, not one Jared tried to explain. I could see and feel the staircase as I walked to the top of the stairs. Jared explained the door at the top of the stairs contained a relaxing space. It was a peaceful and healing space created in my mind. This could be anything I envisioned as calming and relaxing. He then asked me to open the door and walk into my calmness.

My space was a field of bright, colorful wildflowers spread out all around me. In the middle of the flowers was a hammock hanging between two trees. This space was so vivid in my mind that I could have painted the scene on canvas. I would mentally tiptoe through the flowers, climb into my hammock, and lay back into my hypnotherapy session.

After a few weeks of sessions with Jared, I felt more relaxed than ever. He taught me how to escape my reality when my existence felt too heavy. He

A SEEMINGLY UNFILLABLE HEART

taught me how to control my thoughts. While I didn't learn how to manage those thoughts outside of therapy for many years after, the beginning of what would bless me so considerably started in a tiny room with Jared leading the way.

"I have this hole in my heart, this space where Lucy should be. I have spent many years trying to fill the space, but nothing seems to do it." I lowered my head as I spoke to Jared.

It had been seven years since I placed Lucy for adoption, and the hole was not getting any smaller. In 2002, when I gave birth to Jack, I thought my new baby might fill the hole, but it didn't. Then later, when my daughter was born, and I thought I'd feel complete with a baby girl in my arms again. But I didn't. The hole was still there. It grew in size every time I thought I had reached a point where I could fill it with this or that. And the pain only increased every time I tried to pour something into it. It took so much of me—my personality, my thoughts, my time, my energy—to try to fill a bottomless hole.

"Have you ever thought maybe you aren't meant to fill the hole?" Jared asked me.

I eagerly looked up at him and looked him straight in the eye. I was dumbfounded but intrigued. He continued, "You keep trying to fill it, but maybe it isn't meant to be filled."

"I've never thought of that before."

Over the past seven years, I had read books on grief, lost myself serving other birth moms, became a mother, became an adoption advocate, all in the hopes of filling this bottomless void in my heart. And honestly, all of it now seemed silly, like attempts to fill the unfillable. But maybe I wasn't meant to fill this space where Lucy once was. He was exactly right. *How had I missed such a simple concept?* There was no doubt I had a hole in my heart—a genuine and missing part of me that no one, no action could ever fill. That was my reality.

"Maybe accepting you will never fill the hole is the very thing that will heal it," Jared announced.

I never left his gaze. I stared at him in amazement. His words rang true, resonating in every inch of my body. I felt the words hit my chest first and then open my heart. I sat up taller as Jared continued to speak. I had been released. I was no longer carrying the burden of filling the hole in my heart. Light radiated from Jared, to me, and through the crown of my head. In a few short minutes, Jared said what no one had said before, and it made perfect sense.

I began to cry for my nineteen-year-old self who had no idea what this experience would do to her life. I cried in relief. I screamed in frustration. *Why had no one said this to me before? Why was I not guided to this thought from my social worker, LDSFS, the people who were supposed to know and understand the situation better than anyone?* I sobbed and I rejoiced simultaneously, as I had done many times on this adoption journey.

I left Jared's office with a gift more significant than anything I had ever received before. I had permission to move on, to move on with my flawed self, hole in my heart and all. The imperfection I spent years trying to mend was not something I was meant to fix. It is a part of who I am and who I am

A SEEMINGLY UNFILLABLE HEART

meant to be.

I love deeply because I know great loss. I see and feel great light, because I have seen darkness. I appreciate fully, because I know anything can be taken away. Without the contrast in my life, without the imperfections and trials, I wouldn't fully understand the joy and goodness. I was the child that had to burn her finger in order to know the stove was hot. I had to sit in the gunk, appreciate its odor, in order to accept the contrast of beauty surrounding me. I will never regret that life has taught me what I do not want to feel because in learning this, life has also taught me what I do want to have in my life.

Journal Entry — May 7, 2011

To My Beautiful Little Butterfly,

My heart is full today, with love, aching sadness, and unbearable desire to hold you! Today is Birth Mother's Day (the day before Mother's Day). It's a hard day, but a good day full of memories and wishes, memories of your beautiful, precious baby face in my hands, so long ago. I think about your tiny hands and bright eyes and the scent of your baby soft skin, so clear in my mind. If I close my eyes and allow myself to feel you again, tears come rushing. My arms will forever want to hold you, hug you, protect you, and love you. You are a beautiful young lady now, but in my mind the tiny baby is still there, looking up at me.

My wish for you is that you continue to be happy, that your heart will always know of my love, and that you will understand my decision to place you

for adoption. The future will bring us together again, and I pray we will embrace as old friends would.
I pray for you.
I long to see you.
I dream about you.
I hope for you.
I sacrifice for you.
I love you!

XOXO, your birth mom

Journal Entry — August 29, 2013

    Occasionally, I wake to this massive feeling of missing her, my little butterfly. It feels like the weight of the world on my shoulders in an instant. Except no matter what task I check off my list, the weight will not lift. The aching settles inside of my heart making every breath a challenge to exhale from my body. I feel sheepish by my instant reaction to Grief, and all too often, I will curl up in the corner to hide the emotions, even though I know better. Today, I'm choosing to capture Grief.
    I do not know a life any different than the one I have without Lucy. I've never wiped tears from her eyes, helped her brush her hair or even heard her voice. So how is it possible to miss her this profoundly? How is it possible to feel this hurricane of emotions, uncontrollable at the drop of a hat?
    When the weight lifts, and I can inhale with ease, peace finds its way back into my heart. Grief will crawl back into its hiding place and resurface on another day.

A SEEMINGLY UNFILLABLE HEART

Today, I will wipe my own tears, refresh my makeup, and head out the door to meet a friend because I know if I don't continue to marvel at the beauty of a flower, rush to take a photo of a rainbow or use my voice to express my love to those I cherish, Grief will conquer one more victim. But it will not be me.

EIGHT

Post Placement

"Every experience, no matter how bad it seems, holds within it a blessing of some kind. The goal is to find it."
-Buddha

Our quaint rental sat on a half-acre lot at the end of a secluded back road in rural Utah. My oldest son, Jack, was nearly four-years-old when my daughter Ella was three months old. Our kitchen table sat next to a wide window facing out to the front of our house. The kitchen was in the smallest corner, in a house that felt oversized for our family. I loved to wake up and open the thin metal blinds to welcome the sun in. The smell of syrup and the early morning fall air filled the room. Ray had rushed out the door for work before I could finish making breakfast. I made pancakes while cradling Ella in my arms. Jack had his face smashed against the glass, on the kitchen window, watching a few kids line up for the school bus, right outside our house. He watched them every morning as they grabbed their backpacks and raced each other to be the first in line.

"Mom, it's her!" he yelled out.

"It's who, bud?"

"It's Lucy mom. I see her right there! She's waiting for the bus!" Jack said with clear confidence.

I dropped the spatula and hurried to the window. I couldn't help myself. I knew it wasn't her—I knew it wasn't even possible—but my heart leapt at the thought. As I quickly moved, I downplayed my enthusiasm. "It's not her, Jack. She doesn't live here," I said as I eagerly gazed out the window next to him.

Sure enough, there was a young girl, about Lucy's age, with sandy blonde hair and blue eyes who looked a lot like her. The hope inside of me that it could be her, surprised me. I had always wanted to look out the window and see her there, waiting for the school bus. I wanted to hear my son call out her name and wave goodbye with his tiny hand and face smashed against the glass.

"She does look a lot like Lucy, doesn't she?" I stated.

"I thought it was her mom," Jack said disappointedly.

Right there, at the beginning of a mundane day, I had to teach my four-year-old what I was still trying to teach myself. "Someday we may be able to meet

Lucy. It will be a beautiful reunion, and we will all be thrilled to see her. But for now, we have to wait, and we can send her love and light every time we think about her."

I settled Jack in a chair at the table with a plate full of pancakes, put Ella in her high chair, and quietly walked back to our master bedroom. I wrapped my arms around my knees and buried my head into my legs to muffle the sounds of my crying.

My sweet boy was so eager to meet his sister. But frankly, I didn't know if we would ever meet her. I had to come to grips with that possibility the minute I said goodbye to her. I learned that morning that I needed to teach my children the same patience I was trying to develop myself—to wait for something, that may never happen.

Having Jack and Ella brought a chain of events that highlighted what I had missed with Lucy. With each new milestone, I felt joyous and heartbroken. I felt immense gratitude to be their mother, and I sat with that energy a lot, but I also felt like something, someone was always missing.

Journal Entry — June 29, 2010

Dear Lucy,

Ella turned five-years-old in February. It's incredible how much she is starting to look like you. Ella will randomly ask me questions about you, and where you are. She wants to know if we will ever get to meet you. Even at such a young age, I can sense her frustration of wanting to know you, her only sister. We have never kept you a secret from Jack and

Ella, they have always known about you. I catch them looking at your picture on my nightstand. Ella seems the most curious right now, and Jack seems the most content with it.

You are unquestionably a part of who I am and what I do. I'm even more interested in who you are as Ella and Jack get older. I wonder about your school, your friends, your hobbies, and your personality. Many times, I think about running into you, and if you would recognize my face from the one photo you have of me. I even think about silly things like what your swimming suit looks like or what you like to eat. I'm missing you, that's all.

XOXO, your birth mom

"You gave away my only sister!"

Ella's words pierced through my heart. There was honesty in her statement and resentment that couldn't be softened by my reply. Ella was frustrated, upset, and too young to understand the why behind my decision to place Lucy for adoption. Ella was only eight-years-old, at the time, a middle child between two brothers: Jack, who was then ten, and Beau, who is six years younger than Ella. The distress on Ella's face when the technician read our ultrasound and announced she would soon be a big sister to a baby brother was like watching someone pop her most prized balloon. Her hopes of having a sister floated away.

Our children have always known I placed Lucy for adoption. There was no secrecy around this topic.

Often this led to unexpected and uncomfortable questions, but never have I doubted our choice to be upfront with them, at a young age. We discussed where she lived, what she enjoyed, and in simple terms, why I placed her for adoption. There were many times their questions led to a lot of heartache and other moments full of great joy. But today, I found myself speechless as Ella stormed off yelling, "You gave away my only sister!"

She was right, and there was nothing I could do to take away the resentment or give her the experience of having a sister. Ella was all girl— she loved to shop, paint her nails, do make-up, style hair, dance, sing, and embrace everything pink. Ray and I had experienced three miscarriages before we were blessed with Beau. I longed for her to have a sister as much as she ached for one.

I walked out to the backyard and cried out in frustration. *How do I respond to this? How do I help Ella understand when I am still trying to understand it myself?* I cried for the loss of Ella's three siblings who never made it into this world. I cried for Ella—I wanted to take the pain away and to reply with something compelling, but I only felt helplessness. This had become a familiar feeling as a mother, mostly with regard to Lucy and adoption. I was not prepped on how to handle questions from young children about their sibling who was placed for adoption. I was forced to go with my gut when responding to each new situation or question.

As I stood outside and stewed, I heard the sliding glass door open, and Ella's tiny feet came running towards me. As I held her in my arms, I realized she too was grieving. Ella was mourning the loss, as I was, and I never thought about how my decision, so many years ago, would affect my children. Placing Lucy for adoption rippled through my entire family, and together we all experienced great love and significant loss. My job, as Ella's mother, was to guide her through her process of grief, even while I was drowning in it myself.

I held Ella tighter, tears rolling down my face, and I said, "I miss her too. I'm sorry."

Five years after this moment, Ella is now a strong and independent young lady. We talk in more depth about adoption, birth mothers, and Lucy. She doesn't remember screaming those words to me, but it changed how I reacted to my children's questions and concerns. It changed the way we talk about adoption in our home, and it prepared me for the more mature questions my children continue to ask. I am grateful for experiences like this that have taught my family to love unconditionally and wholeheartedly.

Dear Pre-Birth Mother Me,

This path you're about to start on is a long and tedious road. You will wake up from nightmares, cry tears of emptiness, and ache to be whole again. You will experience the most powerful and emotional rollercoaster in this life called Grief. You will sacrifice and give away a part of you that cannot be filled with any worldly treasure, yet you'll continue to try and fill the unfillable. You will know loss, and you will know pain. Birthdays and holidays will

A SEEMINGLY UNFILLABLE HEART

haunt you. When you least expect it, you'll buy a front row seat to the rollercoaster you wish would forget about you. You'll find yourself searching for meaning, purpose, strength, and connection. The great news is that you get the choice to either let the weight swallow you up or become someone your baby will be proud of.

Your due date is drawing near. Your nerves are on edge. As scary as delivering sounds, becoming a mother seems even more frightening. The sweat, the tears, the sacrifice will all make sense once you hear your baby cry. Your eyes will meet hers and somehow, someway, you find yourself loving deeper than you ever thought possible. Your heart will swell, and you'll think, "How will I let you go?" You'll snuggle your heaven-sent angel in your arms, and suddenly, the world makes sense. This life makes sense. You'll question your decision. You'll plead with a higher power to keep her. You'll wonder how you made something so cute and perfect. You will feel pride on a whole new level. Welcome, you are officially a mother.

A hospital bed has never felt more like home. You'll want to plant roots there, only because you know what comes next. Placement day will creep up on you, and you'll wonder, "How will I let you go?" Memorize every inch of the tiniest body you've ever seen. Take a deep breath and hold on for the ride of your life. Your body will do all of the work. It will walk you through step by step. You, my precious soul, will be floating above watching your body take control. And there is nothing wrong with that. Do whatever you need to answer the echoing question,

"How will I let you go?"

Don't rush the process. The timeline of when this takes place is all up to you. This is your time to be selfish. Yes, be selfish. Feed her, watch her sleep, change her, dress her, and anything else that calls on your motherly heart. When people ask you if you have any children, it's okay to say yes. Enjoy the cherished moment of seeing her parents hold her for the first time. Marvel in the beauty of how the Universe brought you all together. Find the joy in the pain. I promise it is there. Keep looking.

The first night without her will feel unnatural, impossible, and more intense than anything you have felt thus far. Cry, scream, sleep, and repeat. This will pass. It will get easier. When people tell you, it will get easier, and you want to punch them in the face, don't. They're right. You find a way to ride the emotional rollercoaster with ease. Welcome, you are officially a birth mother.

You'll fit her in your life in a nontraditional way, and she will thank you for it someday. Your love for her will only grow stronger by the minute. Don't bother filling the hole in your heart, where she belongs—it's unfillable. The sooner you accept its existence, the sooner you will feel whole again. Let it be just that, a hole in your heart. You can still breathe, and you can always love. Don't wait seven years to come to this reality.

Who you become now is whom she will meet later on. Who do you want to be? Make her proud. Make yourself proud. Be guided, as you have this entire journey. Love yourself as significantly as you love her. The sooner you do, the easier life becomes.

A SEEMINGLY UNFILLABLE HEART

You will have negative trolls who question your decision. You'll want to listen to them, don't. Don't let those things you cannot control, control you. Stand tall, always, know you made the best decision for your baby at that time. This choice is nothing to be ashamed of. You, my darling, are becoming what you are meant to be.

The road is long and tedious, but with such opposition comes a deeper understanding of love. One without the other cannot be as profoundly appreciated. Take the dark days to remind you how bright the good days can be. Your life will become what you have always wished for. Accept you are stronger, you are courageous, and you will be a beacon for others. Shine bright and be proud of who you are.

Love, Gina

NINE

Happy Birthday

"If you light a lamp for someone else it will also brighten your path."-Buddha

Happy 9th Birthday – October 5, 2009

Happy Birthday! It's a big day for you. I thought about you a lot on Saturday, October 3. I was thinking you might have had a birthday party with your friends that day.

We celebrate your birthday every year with a cake. We sing happy birthday, and Jack and Ella help me blow out the candles. This year we celebrated with Ray's family. We were at a baseball game together and decided we should all get soup and donuts. We gathered at Ray's sisters' house. Ray's mom and dad were also there. We put together a donut tower and put nine candles in it. We sang happy birthday, and all of the kids blew out the candles.

I am six weeks pregnant with our third child. My mother-in-law, sister-in-law, and I sat around and talked about baby names. We are overjoyed to welcome another child. Every time I get pregnant, I think about my pregnancy with you. I was so sick, and I worked late nights at Old Navy. I would often hide in a dressing room, too nauseous to move, and sit on the small bench surrounded by the clothes I was supposed to be hanging up. I also worked at a preschool with my sister-in-law during the day. I was an aid during the lunch hour. One day it was 115 degrees. I thought my skin was going to melt off of my body.

I am so curious about what you like to do and what type of personality you have. Right now, Ella is taking dance, and sometimes as I watch her, wonder if you love to dance as well. I grew up dancing. I started dancing at the age of nine with a dance group called, The Stars.

I was also on the drill team for three years during high school. I did it more for the social activity, but I have always wished I had taken it more seriously. I loved dancing, and I believe that it is through dance that I discovered my passion for music. I can't play an instrument, but I enjoy the poetry in song lyrics and love searching out new bands.

I wonder what type of birthday party you had and which friends you invited. I think about you being a big sister and how loving you must be. I am the youngest in my family, so I never had the chance to be a big sister. I often wear a locket with your picture in it. It has two charms with the initials E and J alongside it. Ella is four-years-old now. She asked me why her picture wasn't in the locket. I told her it's because I get to see her face every day, and I don't get to see yours. She nodded in agreement.

I am unable to send you letters, but there are many things I want to say to you. I want you to have a record of how meaningful you are in our lives. We all love you and think of you often. We like to celebrate your birthday, and it has become a day we all enjoy together even though you are not here with us.

My mom and I hang out every year on your birthday. We go shopping or out to lunch. Sometimes she will simply come over to my house and sit with me. It is nice to have her close. My mother cares for you and is sensitive to everything associated with your placement. Ray is, too, as he has watched me grieve and celebrate every year. He has lived every up and down with me. You have a special place in all of our hearts. I hope and pray this journal someday finds you, whether that is when you and I finally meet, or when this is sent to you somehow. I pray my eyes will rest upon your beautiful face once again. I pray I get the chance to meet you and get to know you.

You are not forgotten! You are loved doubled, thought about doubled, and I hope this journal is a record of that. You are always in my heart!

XOXO, your birth mom

Journal Entry – October 6, 2009

I miscarried our baby. I wake up every morning thinking about her. I felt strongly she was a girl. I was due on June 3rd, my birthday, and my heart feels broken. Again. It has been tough, mainly because it is so close to your birthday and I always feel more sensitive during this time of year. I wonder if our family is already complete, but I ache to give Jack and Ella another sibling. I will think about this precious angel baby of mine, every year on my birthday.
I hope you are enjoying your birthday gifts. I love you very much!

XOXO, your birth mom

Happy 10th Birthday — October 5, 2010

Dear Lucy,
Our time together was not long, but you left an everlasting print on my heart. I hear your laughter in my dreams and see you becoming much more than that little, precious baby. Remember your birth mother loves you more than words can ever express!

XOXO, your birth mom

Happy 11th Birthday — October 5, 2011

My Little Butterfly,
It was eleven years ago today when they placed you in my arms. You were more beautiful than I had ever imagined. You see, we had a short time

together, not quite nine months, and your delivery day marked the beginning of the end of our time together. It was a bittersweet day for my family and me because we knew it wouldn't be long before we would be saying goodbye, when we had only just said "hello." I held you in my arms and heard the words, "This is not your baby." These words stung me to the core and caught me off guard, but yet their truth rang in my heart. I knew I was called as a pathway for you to come to this earth.

My love for you was intense, and like nothing I had ever felt before. Placing you for adoption has been my biggest lesson and trial in my life! I can't imagine not being your birth mother; it is who I am now. I am a birth mother and more importantly, your birth mother.

The days after you were born went by in a flash. I felt outside of myself. I felt like I was watching the world around me pass by like a movie. I was taking steps, but I didn't feel my feet on the ground. It rained every day I was in the hospital with you. I would watch it from my window and think, *how could anyone understand how I am feeling right now? No one does. No one ever will.* But I was wrong. There were many birth mothers out there who were placing babies for adoption. They were there, but I had no idea. I felt alone and angry. I kept thinking, *Why me? Why can't I keep her?* In my heart, I knew the answer, but I was afraid.

The ride home without you, with the empty car seat sitting next to me, was excruciating. You were now in the arms of a loving father, who just a moment before, looked at his baby girl for the first time. Your relationship with him is one of the reasons why I placed you for adoption. Being a daddy's girl is something I cherish, and I know you will too.

Eleven years ago, my precious little butterfly, I made a decision I can never take back. A decision I spend many hours thinking about, even eleven years later. Your baby face is still forever in my mind, my heart, and my soul. You are a part of who I am!

I can't wait to laugh with you, cry with you, and spend hours talking to you. We will talk about life, love, and everything in between. I know it won't be long now.

You are loved, my little birthday girl. You have many people who have never even met you, who pray for you daily and can't wait to see your beautiful face again. Always feel my love and remember me. I can't wait to say hello again. Happy birthday my precious butterfly! We all love you!

XOXO, your birth mom

Happy 13th Birthday — October 4, 2013

I remember my 13th birthday. My parents took me and a friend to Las Vegas.

I remember telling my parents, "Now that I'm officially a teen, I need like a legit teen party. How about Vegas?"

We spent the weekend in Las Vegas, and my parents escorted us around. It was a fun and memorable trip. I've been thinking about that birthday for a few weeks now. I have even contemplated what I would tell my thirteen-year-old self now that I have traveled twenty years ahead. Would I ask her to stop wanting to grow up so fast? Would I tell her to run? Would I tell her to dream bigger?

I know I would tell her this—don't waste your time creating drama or being involved with drama! Life is too short. Don't assume being in the middle of a soap opera makes you important. It doesn't. It makes for unnecessary heartache, and heartache will come on its own. You are important without the drama.

I would tell her to run, but maybe not in the way you have in mind. Run to whatever is beautiful, positive, enlightening, and brings you joy. Run to it! Run with vigor. Run with freedom. Don't wait for it to come to you. Take charge and run towards what you want and believe in, regardless of what others think.

Dream! Dream bigger, more extensive, and to infinity. If you believe you can, you can! The Universe will bring you your dreams, but they will not simply be given to you. You have to work hard and sacrifice and never lose sight of your dreams.

I would also tell my thirteen-year-old self the path ahead is rough. Heartache is ahead. Trials are ahead. And there will be days when you think you cannot carry yourself into one more day. You will want to give up. You will want to say "Poor me. Why me?" Don't!

Allow yourself to feel every emotion. Allow the sadness, the pain, the beauty, the joy, the grief, and the peace. Live in it, experience it, but don't let the negative bring you down. Don't give it power. Remember everything in life has contrast—good vs. bad, light vs. dark, love vs. hate. Without opposition, and the experience of both sides, you would never appreciate all that is beautiful in life. If you never experience what hurts how would you know what feels good? Learn from each emotion and use them to power positive energy that will surround you when you are strong enough to turn your focus towards it. Use the contrast to raise you up.

The most important thing is love. Love with all of your heart. I have never regretted the love I have given, not one single time, and many times that love has left me heartbroken. But even so, love unconditionally. Don't hold back love, and love will always find you.

Lucy, my little butterfly, turns thirteen tomorrow. The reality is that I want to take her to Vegas for her birthday. I want her to get all dressed up so I can take her out and spoil her rotten. Maybe not so much with money or materialistic items, but with my love, my time, and my words that have gone unheard for thirteen years. I want to show her my world here! I want to share the beautiful things I have discovered and have grown to love. I want her to spoil me with every word she has ever wanted to say and tough questions she has longed to ask. I want her to share her dreams and show me what she has grown to love. I would soak in every pause, every breath, and every word.

I know taking Lucy to Las Vegas for her birthday is not an option. I mean, I can't even buy her a gift. This truth brings mounds of frustration! The lack of control is torturing. I can't change it. I can't love enough, give enough, serve enough or pay anyone enough to change any of it. It is what it is. There is nothing beautiful or profound about that. It's my reality. I can't even sing her happy birthday. I can't do anything!

Instead, I will complete my annual birthday post and journal entry, and pray someday Lucy will see all of this. Lucy will know of my love for her. Lucy will see the frustration. Lucy will hear the raw emotion of what a birth mom goes through on a day-to-day basis. And maybe, just maybe, it will help her understand.

For now, I'm going to embrace each feeling and soak in the contrasting emotions, because I know it's all for my good. I will not feel shameful if I want to cry or if I want to smile. I will not feel shameful if I want to scream out in frustration or share love. Once I am done, and I feel like myself again, I'm going to make my travel plans to Vegas and celebrate!

Journal Entry — September 12, 2016

I have been hiding in a dark place. I have moments of light and hopeful thoughts, but then I'm swallowed back into the thickness of Grief.

Yes, Grief, sixteen years later. How is it possible? I wish I could answer this question. There is a twinge of shame, making me hesitant to write this because it's the same damn thing every year.

I thought this year was going to be different. I felt stronger, less emotional, present enough in my life to be able to "catch it" before it caught me. But that's the funny thing about Grief. He is sneaky. He is unpredictable. I hate that Grief still finds me all of these years later. I should have this figured out by now. He creeps into my daily life, as I battle not feeling "good enough." No matter how hard I try, when Grief pays his visit, I can't see any of the good that I do. Grief highlights the failures and disappointments in my life. I know that all I have to do is put my boxing gloves on and remind myself I have beat Grief before, but this year I feel weak. I felt defeated before he crept his way into my thoughts.

It's written all over my face, but yet I still try to ignore it, push it aside, and lie my way through my days. But I'm exhausted. I know I thought this year would be different, that Grief was not coming for me, but he did, and I can't hide it anymore. And why should I?

Instead of lying to those around me, creating a false impression for fellow birth mothers, and all of my friends and family who have suffered Grief along with me, I should shout it out, "Here I am, in all my Grief-stricken glory!" I'm struggling with this inevitable change of seasons that I both love and dread. I'm not the best mom, wife, friend, sister, co-worker or human right now, and that's okay.

And yet I still struggle in being honest with my journey. I'm not myself today — I'm a little down — and I can't seem to fight the negative thoughts in my head right now. But as always, I refuse to be ashamed or hide from my reality. This is me right now — this is me today. Tomorrow might be better, and it might not, and that's okay too. In a society that focuses on perfection, I'm going to voice my faults and raw emotions because I know I am learning, and vulnerability is a part of my journey.

To a birthday girl who will be sixteen in three weeks, I'm still here. I'm still as imperfect as the day I placed you for adoption, but today I'm not ashamed of who I am like I was before. I hope you are learning to love yourself as much as you love others. I hope when you have days of darkness that you allow yourself to feel, learn, grow, and let go. Not one single day has passed without a thought of you. I love you dearly and can't wait for the day of sweet embrace.

Now excuse me while I go make myself a shirt that says, "kicking Grief's ass, one day at a time" aka five-thousand eight hundred and forty days, to be exact.

Happy 16th Birthday — October 5, 2016

I'll admit, when my alarm went off this morning, I pulled the covers high above my head and wished this day away. I want to put my headphones on, drown myself in depressing music, and sleep. Healthy, right?

Instead, I rolled out of bed, an hour after my alarm went off, and noticed that Jack, my fourteen-year-old, had slept in too. I rushed to wake him up, ironed his shirt, and made three lunches. I brewed coffee and waited for the kids to leave for school. I needed to release these intense feelings all alone.

I'm angry. I'm sad. I'm cranky. I'm highly

emotional. I feel lonely. I'm exhausted. This is what the ring looks like when you're fighting with Grief! And all I want to do is go back to the version of me who was tackling my job, juggling mommy life, and feeling balanced. Pardon me while I cry, kick, scream, and throw a tantrum in this ring. I have to release this energy.

I have one million things to do today before I leave for Pinners Conference, ironically in the state where Lucy lives. I am presenting for the company I work for, Close to My Heart. I need my A-game this weekend. I can't be tinkering with Grief right now, but Lucy is turning sixteen today and I want nothing more than for her to have a fabulous day. I know she is loved. I know she is healthy. I know she wants to become a lawyer someday. I know she's a trendsetter. I know she is witty. I know she is strong. I know she is my little butterfly. I'm going to hold onto those positive, happy thoughts, and beat Grief so I can go on with my day.

Happy birthday, my beautiful butterfly! I promise I will sing and celebrate after I finish this tantrum.

XOXO, your birth mom

Journal Entry — September 28, 2017

To My Little Butterfly,

You are not so little anymore. You will turn seventeen-years-old next week. It has been six thousand, two hundred and five days since I held you last. It feels like day three! If I could turn back time, I would spend one more day with you, until one more day turned into hundreds and then thousands of days. It's easy for me now to wish you were here, sitting next to me, as I type my innermost hopes and dreams for you. I want to look over and see your angelic face looking back at me. I'd see seventeen years of wiped tears, encouragement, friendship, love, and memories. I long for that to be our story, but it's not.

Our story is one of sacrifice, selflessness, unconditional love, and a gift. Our story has placed hundreds of miles between us, from the time you were four days old. I can't look into your eyes and see years of memories. I can't pretend to know who you are or who you want to become. However, I can look in the mirror and see you there, and I can see you in every memory I have over the past seventeen years.

I see long nights full of tears and anguish. I see nightmares and remember the subconscious fear that someone or something would take my second born child. I see you in every gift basket, shared with a grieving birth moms. I see you in every instance when I shared our story, at hundreds of adoption conferences, retreats, high schools, and support groups. I see you in her, my third child, a beautiful baby girl. I see days of teaching my children about you, about adoption, about Grief, and about patience. I see yearly birthday cakes frosted with a wave of emotions. I see a family who loves and adores you. I see years of learning about who I am, without you.

No other moment in my life has shaped me more

than letting you go. No other moment has taught me more about myself, about becoming a mother, and about selfless love. You see, my little butterfly, it may have been six thousand, two hundred and five days since I last held you but it hasn't been seventeen years since I loved you last!

As you turn seventeen-years-old and you begin to discover yourself and prepare to be on your own, I hope you'll look back and know, without a doubt, I was always with you.

Be confident! Do not shy away from why you were brought into this world — to share your passion and love for others. Find your passion! Look within, search your soul, and live out your dream. Believe in the impossible! No mountain is too high, no goal is too hard, no task is too big. You can achieve anything. Believe in your power. Love yourself, my little butterfly. Talk nicely to yourself. Be kind to yourself. Remember your worth.

XOXO, your birth mom

Happy 17th Birthday — October 5, 2017

Today is your big day. My first thought was, once again, *Do I have to get up?* I want the beginning of this day to be the end. I wish I were climbing in bed and saying "goodnight" rather than "good morning." I would know then that I had conquered and survived the day. I could move on with other thoughts. I feel guilty for wanting the day to slip away. I should be thrilled to wake and celebrate a beautiful day, a birthday. The cake is ready, plans are made, and all I want to do is lie in bed.

This year has been difficult, but I am also on an ascent of learning about myself. I have been stripped down to the bones of who I am, how strong I can be, and where I go from here. But all of this has made year seventeen a bit tricky.

I may not answer my calls or texts today, but please know that I will see my friends and family and will acknowledge the love I have for you. I will take these thoughts and feelings to a place where I know they will be heard — the mountains.

The support I've had all of these years has been priceless to me. I don't know if many of my fellow birth moms receive such unconditional love and support. I know I am fortunate.

In light of it all, I could be nearing "the end" of the beginning, as you near eighteen-years-old. I want to sit and marvel in it, but after all this time, I know better than to allow such hopes.

I've been asked a lot of questions today by my children, who ache to know you and to be a part of your life. Questions that I don't know how to answer. Questions I've asked for seventeen years now. Frustration overcomes me when I am not able to teach them how to handle these thoughts.

Regardless, the day will carry on. The sun will rise here shortly. We'll light the candles, and we'll sing the song, and I will be wishing and waiting for "the end." The end of today and most of all the end of my years celebrating your birthday all alone.

We love you very much, my little butterfly. I know you will soar today with such beauty and grace. We are all in awe of you and who you're becoming. We ache to know more about you and to see you. May this birthday bring you love, light, and spoiled rottenness.

XOXO, your birth mom

TEN

The End of A Fairytale

"Someone I loved once gave me a box full of darkness. It took me years to understand that this, too, was a gift."
-Mary Oliver

"*We* need to talk tonight when I get home."
Ray called on his lunch break from work to make sure I was going to be home for his serious announcement. I chuckled in response. He was so stern and serious that it sounded to me like a joke. When he didn't appear to see the humor, I hung up thinking I had done something wrong and started a mental-checklist of all of the things it might be. I was pregnant with our third child, Beau. After two

miscarriages, resulting in two D&C's (Dilation and Curettage), we were shocked when we found out I was pregnant again. I was due in three months.

I was standing in the foyer of our home when Ray got home. He walked in, head hung low, and every horrible scenario went racing through my mind.

"Let's go upstairs please," he whispered.

He followed me as I waddled up the stairs to our master bedroom. I sat awkward and uncomfortable on the edge of our king size bed. Ray sat right across from me, on the zebra printed couch, the one I fell in love with at Ikea. Each scenario that fit the demographics of this situation were not good. Why wasn't he sitting beside me? Why didn't he kiss me when he walked in the door?

"Shawn called me today at work." He said it slow and precise, yet I found myself already one step behind his words. "He has always kept track of where we are, in case he needed to get a hold of us." His words were trailing off into blank spaces above our heads.

I rested my hands on my massive belly and started crying in apprehension. My thoughts went to the worst possible scenarios. *Did Lucy pass away? Was she in a horrible accident? Was she alive?* These questions were screaming in my head, but I sat in silence, cold and still. Every hair stood on edge. Every cell in my body vibrated. Every inch of who I was and who I would become thereafter, knew from this point forward nothing would feel the same.

"Shawn and Alice are getting divorced."

A deep inhale, and a sigh of relief first settled in

my body. Lucy was okay. She was healthy, and she was alive. My fleeting comfort turned to tears, and my tears became sobs. Ray paused, he was also tearful and waiting for a break in my emotions, but nothing stopped me, as ten years of grief and sorrow collapsed any resistance I had left. The echoing of our tears vibrated through the walls around us. Ray's very sensitively watched me swallow and then choke on the information, as I sat there in sheer disbelief that what I tried to shield her from was now her reality. There was no blocking my devastation. The fairy-tale life I believed I had given her was abolished. I rocked myself back and forth, like a child, as Ray came over to comfort me.

Once we had exhausted all conversation, I laid drained and quivering on our bed. Ray flipped the lights off as he walked out of the bedroom, shutting the door behind him. The sheets high on my head, my arms wrapped around my shins, and my legs tucked as close to my belly as possible. I ran through thoughts of disbelief and shame. Coincidentally, I faced the same thoughts my father did when I told him I was pregnant. *I have failed her. I have a child with a major challenge, and I need to be there for her.* Unlike my parents, I couldn't assist Lucy in finding her way.

I had promised her a life with a happy ending, and I failed at keeping that promise. I had hundreds of parent profiles to pick from, and pleas from families who wanted this baby girl. I shut them all down and single-handedly picked the couple who was now getting divorced. I was clear about my desire to place because I didn't want to see my baby live in two separate houses, with two separate parents. I was giving her the castle in the sky—a mother and a father who could give her what I couldn't give her.

Shawn and Alice were supposed to step in and fill that space in her life. Where I was unable, they were able. Where I was weak, they were to be strong. Where I couldn't give, they were to provide. *Were my expectations unrealistic?* Did I create this apparently perfect adoptive life for her in my own head, or was that actually what I signed up for from the beginning? The life I thought I had given her was gone.

Advocating for adoption had been my main focus for the past ten years. How would I stand in front of crowds now and confidently say I did the right thing? The script I had rehearsed and spoken in front of thousands of people felt like a lie. I believed I placed my baby girl in a better situation than what I could give her. Gullible, I believed in the fairy-tale ending. I shouted my decision to place my baby for adoption from the highest rooftops when other birth parents were not speaking out. Now, I didn't believe in anything. I didn't believe in adoption, and I didn't believe in my choice. I didn't believe in divine inspiration. I didn't believe in myself.

Years of advocating for something I now felt such hatred toward made me feel phony. I would never stand on the adoption stage again with such conviction. The certainty was gone. I was robbed of the only truth I still believed. I was bound in the ropes of the LDSFS voices, "You're making the best decision for your baby. You're doing the right thing." I felt safe in those words. They were reassuring when days were impossible. They were guidelines for me to rely on. The Grief, the pain, the loneliness, the post-traumatic stress, they were all consequences of an action that was worth the effects. The ropes of a fairy-tale were my safety net, and now they were cut and unraveling at my feet. My first reaction was to reach down and tie them back together, wrapping each loop under and over my arms and legs, as if they would hold in the sting of regret.

My thoughts raced recklessly. For the first time, I thought about getting Lucy back. I wanted to bring her home, to a space I had worked hard to create, to a marriage I fought hard to keep together. I envisioned her with us and how she would be awaiting the arrival of a new baby brother. I thought about what room she would have picked out in our new home, and how she would fit perfectly into our family center. These thoughts were no different than what I had thought every day before, but now, I wanted nothing more than her flesh and blood to be right next to me. I was resentful, angry, and frustrated with a situation I had chosen. I couldn't control it—I never could—and this divorce compounded those helpless feelings. I abandoned every positive belief surrounding my placing Lucy for adoption.

I fell in and out of consciousness between sobs, pregnancy hormones, a sense of failure, and shock. The following morning, I woke up to one daunting question.

"Oh my God, how will I tell my parents?"

After all of these years, I once again found myself

with the frightening chore of telling my parents something unpleasant. I felt most protective of my mother. I often had to process any information regarding Lucy before I shared it with my mom. It wasn't because of her lack of support, but rather my own desire to comfort her if ever she found information troubling or overwhelming. I did this with the most straightforward details. I had to enter each conversation with my mother with a steady front. I had to categorize my reactions and thoughts to every letter I received before I could adequately share them with anyone in my life, even Ray. It was my way of getting a small measure of control in an uncontrollable situation. If I felt okay with what was shared, those around me would feel okay about it as well. I could help guide them through their feelings because I had already found a positive place for them to rest. My confidence was contagious in every aspect of my decision.

My letters from Shawn and Alice were pleasant, but bringing up Lucy with those around me shined a spotlight on a story plagued with sadness and frustration for my entire family. The time I needed to process was different in each situation, with each letter, but I had a feeling that this announcement was going to shatter everyone's idealistic castle in the sky where we believed Lucy lived.

There was no positive space for me to digest this information before I shared it with my parents. I could not find the confidence before I spoke because I had lost my very reason for placing Lucy for adoption. I feared that others would judge not only me, but my mother, as they had during my

A SEEMINGLY UNFILLABLE HEART

pregnancy. Friends, family, and church members often asked her why she was allowing me to place my baby for adoption. These people disapproved of my decision and of her supportive hand. I was now concerned that Shawn and Alice's divorce was another mark in their favor as to why I should have parented Lucy.

I pulled away from my work with Birth Mother Baskets. I canceled basket orders, speaking engagements, and in one swift instant, the word "adoption" held for me the same ugliness and frightening chills as saying, "Lord Voldemort." I wanted to lie in bed forever and envision Lucy's holy land of rainbows and, of course, butterflies. I wanted to erase everything I heard and go back to my naïve belief that when you place a baby for adoption, your baby lives on happily ever after. But I couldn't!

I became increasingly grateful for the baby boy I was now carrying. His journey to get to us had followed two failed pregnancies, and now I understood why. My unborn son was the main reason I continued to get up every morning. He was the reason I didn't give up on taking care of myself. I couldn't wallow in the regret I was now sinking in. I had responsibilities as a mother to Ella who was five-years-old and Jack who was eight-years-old, and to Beau who would be coming in four short months. I bowed out of birth mom support groups and kept a lower profile than what I was accustomed too. The truth was, I didn't know what to say to my fellow birth mothers and the adoption community. So I said nothing.

Months later, I woke up in the middle of the

night recollecting a conversation I had with my oldest sister, Anna. We had met to have lunch together at a local restaurant before Shawn and Alice got divorced. Anna was driving me to her house, where my car was parked. As we were driving, she started talking about her high school friend who had adopted her oldest son. She told me that her friend was now getting divorced. Anna found this so sad, and she couldn't stop thinking about this boy's birth mother and what she must be feeling. I had forgotten about this conversation until that night. As Anna spoke, I contemplated how horrible it would be. The epiphany sent chills up my spine. I often think back on that conversation and wonder if the Universe was preparing me, and maybe if I had only gotten the hint, I would have adapted more easily.

After the initial blow, Shawn started emailing us frequently. I even received emails with recordings of Lucy's voice. I heard more about her than I had heard in years. I can't say the good outweighed the bad because there were also emails full of hurt. Shawn's world was being turned upside down, and there was a lot of resentment on his side. I found it much more productive to have Ray read the emails first. He would distinguish what I "needed to know" from what I "didn't need to hear." I don't know what I would have done without him deciphering emails appropriately. There was no one better who knew what I could handle and what would swallow me whole.

I attended my first adoption conference months after the divorce and spoke with a social worker who worked with LDSFS. He was not a part of my placement, but I confided in him for advice. After his speech, I approached him and told him that Lucy's parents were in the middle of a divorce. He did not give me any eye-opening advice, but one thing he said stuck with me: He told me only 10% of adoptive parents get divorced. Only ten percent! Nothing else sunk in from that conversation other than the fact that I managed to pick one of the ten percent of couples. I walked away thinking, *Why did he tell me that? What purpose does it serve? Was the statistic supposed to make me feel better or worse?* Because I definitely felt worse. I was coming to him in a vulnerable state, with my soft-spoken words and tears, as I tried to explain my current situation. He even responded with his back towards the classroom of birth moms, in a low voice, as if he didn't want my "unrealistic" story to ooze out to the "happily ever after" birth mothers behind us. I left my first adoption conference, post-divorce, in tears. I blamed myself for picking what was in my mind the one and only divorced adoptive couple in the entire world. I learned two things from this conversation with "Mr. LDSFS":

1. Just because you are brave enough to share your most sacred moments with others doesn't mean it will be followed with sincerity and open arms. Don't get me wrong, I had many opportunities where being authentic and open helped me heal deep wounds, but those were moments where I wasn't "expecting" a healing situation. Share because you know that by just saying the words out loud, you will feel relief. Don't expect others'

responses to soothe you—there is no magic in their words. The magic is in your power to voice them.

2. 40-50% of marriages in the United States end in divorce, and though I believed Mr. LDSFS at the time, I doubt adoptive couples are a minority to this statistic.

I hate the expression—time heals all wounds, especially when it comes to Grief, but in this situation, I agree. The divorce took a real toll on my decision to place. The reality was that I had put my trust in the hands of strangers and said, "Here. Create the perfect life for my baby." But over time I learned that the Universe doesn't work that way. Life doesn't work that way. We all have trials we must face, and unfortunately some of the lessons we must learn can only be implemented when we go directly through the trial and face it head-on. When we meet trials with this force and eagerness to learn, we come out on the other side brighter and stronger. The divorce was a life lesson for Lucy, just as Ella, Jack, and Beau will have life lessons that I'd prefer to protect them from. But I can't do that, and I'd like to think that I wouldn't even if I could because they must learn. Their strength lies in their ability to adapt. Lucy will find her way through her parents' divorce, as I found my way through her placement.

The divorce forced me to look deeper into why I placed my baby for adoption. I could no longer answer with the poster child response of having given her "more." I had to go to the core of why I made that life-changing decision. *Why did I place Lucy for adoption?*

It all came down to the two positive

confirmations I had during my pregnancy: First, the moment in my truck, listing my mental pros and cons, and second, the precise words I heard when I first held her, "This is not your baby." In truth, this is why I decided to place Lucy for adoption, and no one can take those moments away from me or convince me they never occurred. There is no way for me to communicate the certainty I have from these confirmations. I believe every birth mother has to find a foundation she can cling to in dark times of Grief and scrutiny because every placement will diverge from that fairy-tale feeling at one point or another.

Journal Entry – 2014

I have decided to step away from Birth Mother Baskets. After fourteen years, I am proud of the work I have done and the many birth mothers we were able to reach. I have seen an increase in birth mother's starting their own organizations and speaking their truths, and this brings so much joy to my heart. It has been a humbling experience and a dream to service my fellow birth mothers. When this "aha moment" came to me, I never could have imagined how quickly it would grow, or how deeply people would connect to the idea of showing empathy to birth parents. I hope my efforts have shined a positive light on adoption, especially birth parents, and the unconditional love that we have for our children who are placed for adoption. I hope I was able to change stereotypes and educate others on the importance of post-placement therapy, birth mother connection, and the power of telling your story. I am confidently walking away, as I know there are many organizations that will continue to support and care for birth parents.

I'm enjoying my job as an art consultant, and spending more time with my children. As I close one door, I know I am opening another. I am moving forward with a grateful heart for where I have been. I am diving into my artistic abilities and learning more about the art industry.

Every time I stepped into a store to buy items for the baskets, every fundraiser we put on, every delivery that went out, I thought of Lucy. Over the past fourteen years, BMB has been my connection to Lucy in a way that only I can fully understand. I realize now my connection with Lucy is not only in the baskets I have delivered, but deep within me and her. As I move forward, I know I will always be connected to Lucy, the adoption community, and my fellow birth mothers. I am excited to see what is ahead.

I WAS SURPRISED TONIGHT with the most thoughtful gift I have ever been given, a Birth Mother Basket. My dear friends, who have supported me from day one, invited me out for dinner. When I arrived I was greeted with a canvas photo of Lucy and I, a basket, and handwritten letters from all of them. This group of friends also hosted a "baby shower" for me, while I was pregnant with Lucy. Their genuine love and kindness towards me has carried me through many challenging times in my life.

A SEEMINGLY UNFILLABLE HEART

My Birth Mother Basket was full to the brim with similar items that I had been including in my baskets, but with a special touch from lifelong friends. It was the greatest gift I have ever been given.

G,

Tonight, we wanted to take a minute and honor you with a Birth Mother Basket. You have filled so many birth mothers with hope and with love through your act of service over the past 14 years! We are so proud of you "G." I am grateful to call you a friend of mine. All 12 of us are mothers now, and we understand more fully how big of a sacrifice you have made. We felt the best way to show our love to you was to give you the last and final Birth Mother Basket.

My Dearest Gina Friend,

I just wanted to let you know how incredibly proud I am of you. You have accomplished so much in your life! Each new journey you embark on, I am always amazed at your drive to follow through. I am amazed at the way you dream and how you make your dreams your reality. I have no question that your decision to place Lucy was the right choice for you at that time in your life. I believe it has allowed you to touch others and positively influence others who have had to endure the same kind of pain you have. What an amazing service BMB has been for you and others. You have been such a great example to me of how to give of yourself, time, and talents. Embrace this change and be proud of the good you have accomplished. I love you dear friend!

GINA CROTTS

Dearest Gina,

I have always been so proud of you, my friend. You are truly an unselfish, genuine, loving person. I know that no matter where the future will lead you, you will make a difference, in the lives of those who are lucky enough to know you! I feel extremely lucky to be your friend. I admire you so much. You are true to yourself, and you hold your head high and enjoy life. Thank you for being an example to me. To know you, is to love you!

ELEVEN

The Square

"*Mom,* I know that's not her but the girl standing behind you, in the Brigham Young University (BYU) sweatshirt, looks exactly like Lucy," my daughter, Ella, amusingly says to me. I had not seen Lucy since I placed her for adoption when she was four days old.

Ella and I were at rehearsals for her performance in Sparklepark, an interactive dance party for families. Ella had auditioned among 60+ other dancers to earn her spot in the show. As we drove the thirty minutes to auditions, Ella looked nervous. Neither of us had experienced a dance audition before, and we were unsure what to expect.

"What are they going to ask me to do? Ella asked.

"I'm not sure babe. It will be a great opportunity for you to see how an audition runs." I answered her. Her nerves were high, and I could hear her thoughts reeling, as we got closer to the rehearsal room.

"I'll tell you what, let's at least get there. If you don't want to do it, we'll go shopping or grab an early lunch instead."

I had no intention of letting her skip this audition, but my statement seemed to calm her enough to silence her hidden fears. I checked Ella in, they gave her an audition number, and I stayed as she stretched in the hallway. Ten minutes later they asked for only the dancers to come back into the studio for auditions. Ella looked over at me with excited nervousness.

"You've got this. Be bubbly. Smile. Be confident, and show them why you love to dance," I encouraged her.

I had no expectations as to where this would lead. I merely wanted my daughter, who is aspiring to be a professional dancer, to experience an audition. I waited three hours in the hallway, talking among some of the other parents, as we discussed our children's talents. In the last twenty minutes girls started to leave the studio and walk through the hallway, most of them tearful. It was clear they had started making cuts and sending dancers home. I waited and waited. I did not see Ella come out, and my curiosity led me into the back hallway where auditions were taking place. When I spotted Ella, she was standing in line with sixteen other dancers,

A SEEMINGLY UNFILLABLE HEART

waving to a camera with an accomplished smile on her face.

She made it! I thought to myself. I was shocked, proud, and happy for my beautiful daughter. Once she exited the room, she came right over to me and gave me a big hug.

"I made it mom! I made it!" she was overjoyed.

The next two months we spent many hours driving to and from The Square (a local mall) for rehearsals, in preparation for the two live shows she would be performing in.

This dress rehearsal was her last at The Square. The remainder would be held at the show's location a mile down the road. The large rehearsal room windows faced out to mall shoppers. The room was once a storefront and was now being used as a dance room. During this particular rehearsal, I was sitting inside the dance room with my back to the windows. I could not see people who were walking by. It wasn't unusual to get a few shoppers who would stop and watch the talented dancers, especially on a day like today, as the dancers tried on colorful wigs, costumes, and the music was playing loud.

When Ella approached me, the B-Boys were dancing, and she was on a 5-minute break. Her comment was one I had heard several times from my children. They were always thinking someone looked like Lucy or asking questions about where she lived. These questions and comments were welcomed in our home. With our yearly emails and pictures, my children were also aware of what Lucy looked like, and the communication we had with Shawn and Alice. Ella, at that time, had a picture of

Lucy in her room. The picture was of Lucy and her brother, both three years younger than they would have been on that day.

As Ella spoke, I smiled with curiosity, and as I started to turn around, her comment about this girl wearing a BYU sweatshirt ignited something inside of me. I was aware of Lucy's desire to attend law school at BYU once she graduated from high school, and for the first time, as I turned to look, I thought to myself, *Could it be her, after all of this time?*

TWELVE

A Full Heart

"The Universe is asking...show me your new vibration and I will show you miracles." -Abraham Hicks

I turned back to see Lucy's dad, Shawn. He brought his hands up, palms in the air, and shrugged his shoulders, as if saying "Oh, hey, it's us!" I never saw Lucy's face out there among the mall shoppers. Seeing Shawn's pure shock and bewilderment was all I needed to turn back to Ella and shout, "That's her! That is Lucy!"

Ella responded with an open mouth and silence. I grabbed the nearest leg sitting next to me, another dance mom, and announced, "My daughter that I placed for adoption seventeen years ago is standing out there in the hallway," as if this mom would know what my next move should be. I stood up in a stupor and walked towards the door. I stopped and thought, *I can't go out there. I can't legally approach them.* I wasn't even sure whether that was true.

The door leading out to the mall was not visible from the storefront window. I rested my back on the door. I wasn't blocking it so they couldn't get in, but rather protecting myself. I could not see out, and they could not see me, as I battled in my head over what to do next. The conversation between myself and I continued for a brief moment. I continued debating.

I can't walk out there and see her walking away. My heart and my head cannot hold such a picture. I need to stand here and give them the chance to leave if that is what they wish to do. I need to wait, just a minute, I thought to myself. Shocking haze draped over my face as eternity circled me. When I got enough nerve, and without thought, I peered out the window again and saw Shawn motion towards me to come out into the hallway. My heart leapt.

I turned the knob and took two steps into the hallway before I was standing face to face with Lucy. I reached out and grabbed her without hesitation and pulled her into my chest. My arms wrapped tight around her tiny body. Her oversize BYU sweatshirt engulfed her and so did I. My left hand tight around her waist my right hand resting on her silky, light brown hair. There was no space between us, not thousands of miles, or legal papers saying I could not hold onto her. My baby was now an exquisite young lady right before my eyes, right back in my arms once again, seventeen years later. Every pore in my body combined with hers at that moment, and we were as one. We were connected, as we had always been all of these years.

The seemingly unfillable hole that had unknowingly prompted every decision early in my life, and that had been the source of constant heartache for over a decade, was instantly spilling out unconditional love all around me. The floodgate of every human emotion, the ones that rest shallow beneath a thin layer of skin, waiting for the wick to be lit, was blowing out flames from every pore in my body. I felt it all — The Universe, God the Almighty, I as a whole, Lucy as she is, and everything that had passed before us. I felt whole.

When we finally pulled ourselves apart enough to look at each other face to face, I lifted my hands towards her face and brushed her hair away from her eyes.

"Look at you! Are you happy?" I asked.

"Yes, very happy." She confirmed.

I whispered with the purest intent and motherly nature, "I love you," and pulled her towards me once again.

"I love you too." She whispered back.

Lucy was a few inches shorter than I, due to the wedged boots I was sporting, but there was no denying the apparent similarities between us. We spent a few minutes catching up while meeting some of her family members, her dad, younger brother, younger sister, and a cousin. We all stood there in the drafts of The Square and talked about the mind-blowing reality that we were all face to face. Lucy's younger brother, Nicholas, stood at 6'2" with broad shoulders. He was a gentle giant, like his father. He was unable to hide his amazed, open-mouth shock. As I spoke, I could feel his excitable intent to listen to my every word, as if he were in awe that I was able to talk at all. I would stop mid-sentence and laugh at his inability to hide his emotion, I too unable to refrain from giggling at him. We were all shocked except for Lucy who was calm, poised and delighted.

Shawn turned to me and said, "We're not in a hurry. Would the two of you like to take some time alone?"

My first reaction was nervous excitement. What would I say to her? I had never allowed a reunion to play out in my mind. I would not let my heart be filled with forbidden words. I never imagined this moment, right now, with her, would ever be a reality. I was not prepared.

We walked arm in arm down the mall. After the first hug, we had yet to let go of one another, holding hands, hugging or leaning towards each other enough to be touching. The invisible pull to be next to Lucy was dominant over everything else. Our souls linked together like two magnets after decades apart. Once our line of direction found each other, it was impossible to pull us in opposite ways. No force could split us apart or deny us of the certainty that we were a part of one another.

WE SAT ON A forest green ornate bench, in the middle of the mall. We leaned into each other, our shoulders touching, Lucy's hand resting on mine.

A SEEMINGLY UNFILLABLE HEART

We sat together, two beacons colliding after signaling each other for seventeen years. The draw to be next to her was as deeply in her as it was in me. The energy of our love hammered down self-built walls that were guarded by the mightiest. Without hesitation, I allowed her to crash right into my full heart.

"I just want to look at you," I said.

"I know, me too."

"Let me see your hands and your ears." I marveled at the beauty of her and the reality that I was with her. We took a picture of us with my phone, and both looked down to see our masterpiece.

"We do look a lot alike," Lucy stated.

"I know! Let's text this picture to Ray and see what he says." I laughed. I sent the message, and we both impatiently waited for his reply.

His response, "What?!"

"It's her. It's her," I texted back.

"Tell her to take that BYU sweatshirt off!" Ray is a rival Utah University fan.

Lucy and I both broke out in laughter. I fidgeted with my phone, showing Lucy pictures of her grandparents, cousins, aunts, and uncles. I was in full mom brag book mode, flipping through our family and showing her every single person who has loved her from afar.

"I'm so sorry. I'm probably overwhelming you," I said. I had no idea what the protocol was for this situation. I was acting and reacting solely on my instincts.

"No, you're fine. I love all of them."

"And they love you, so much," I replied.

Lucy was alive. She was happy. She was sitting here with me now, and all I could think about was how I created her. I was in awe of her. Had I never found the courage to go through with the pregnancy, had I chose to get an abortion and let her, and all of it disappear as if nothing happened, she wouldn't be sitting here next to me. The heaviness of regret during my pregnancy, the heartbroken nights getting over her birth father, every ounce of questioning whether I did the right thing, came to a sudden halt. My shameful questioning, in a matter of minutes, turned into a sense of achievement. I felt proud. I wanted to parade her around The Square shouting, "This is my baby! She is my baby!" The motherly instinct that had kicked in automatically when she was born was sparkling around us. I had to refrain from telling every stranger passing by us!

"Look how amazing you are," I blurted out, "I am so proud of you. I love you."

"I never questioned whether you loved me or not. I always knew you did. I always knew you cared about me," Lucy said with such conviction.

I didn't ask her to say it. I never implied I needed to hear it. I was unaware of the yearning I had for her words, as if I had been traveling through the thickest desert sand, thirsty for the exact water I was not allowed to touch, let alone drink. Her words fulfilled a lifetime of cravings and yearning I never knew I wanted. It satisfied the seemingly unfillable parts of who I was. And I thought to myself, *At last, I am full.*

When it was time to say goodbye, I pulled her in once again, like I had a hundred times in the last hour, and said, "I love you. Be a good girl."

A SEEMINGLY UNFILLABLE HEART

As I let go of her, the tears that had been hiding behind shock and delight flooded my face. I looked at her, and her family, and said, "Those are the exact words I said to you the last time I said goodbye. When you were just four days old."

I watched them walk down the hall and out of sight with a chest full of indescribable feelings and a heart filled to the brim.

I sat down next to Ella and the other dance moms in the crowded rehearsal room as we all cried and hugged each other, when a text pinged my phone. It read, "So nice to finally meet you (heart emoji). Let's not make it another seventeen years before we see each other again." Love, Lucy.

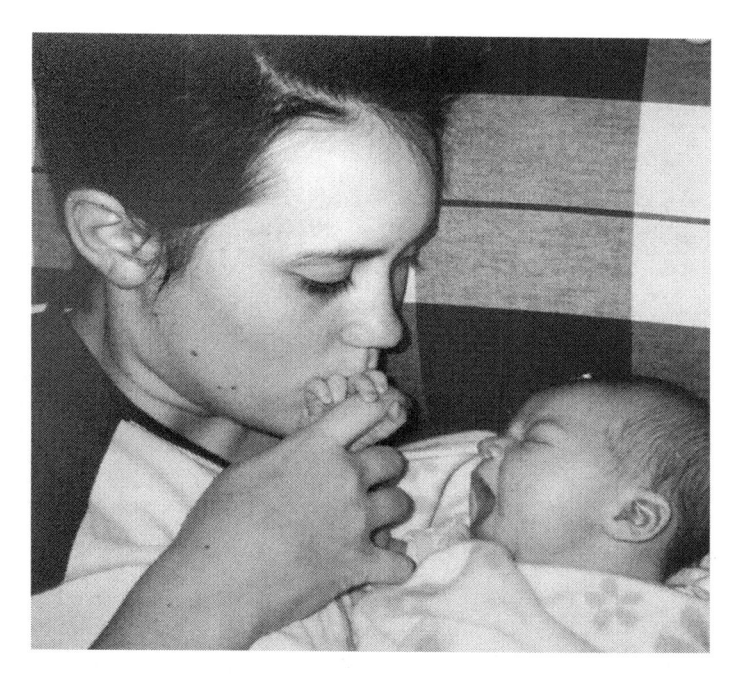

Gina and her little butterfly — Oct. 8, 2000.

ABOUT THE AUTHOR

GINA CROTTS was born and raised in Utah. After placing her little butterfly for adoption in the fall of 2000, Gina founded Birth Mother Baskets. A non-profit organization focused on providing emotional support, to birth mothers post-placement.

After fourteen years of running Birth Mother Baskets, Gina stepped away to pursue a career as a Creative Arts Manager with a local scrapbooking company. A severe concussion in 2016 led Gina back to rediscover her passion for writing.

Currently, Gina works as a Content Writer with CAIRS Solutions where she guides hopeful adoptive couples through their online profile creation.

Gina lives in what she calls her "house in the clouds" with her husband and their three children.

To hear where Gina and her little butterfly are now, visit her website www.ginacrotts.com

Made in the USA
San Bernardino, CA
09 March 2020